Faith
Breaks

Faith
Breaks

*Thoughts on Making
it a Good Day*

J. Howard Olds

Providence House Publishers
PROVIDENCE PUBLISHING CORPORATION
FRANKLIN, TENNESSEE

To the people of Brentwood United Methodist Church
who continue to air *Faith Breaks* and give me
the awesome privilege of serving as their senior pastor.

The lyrics on page 69 are from "Hymn of Promise" by Natalie A.
Sleeth. Copyright ©1986 Hope Publishing Company, Carol Stream,
Illinois, 60188. All rights reserved; used by permission.

Printed in the United States of America

08   07   06   05   04   1   2   3   4   5

Library of Congress Control Number: 2004107476

ISBN: 1-57736-320-5

Cover design by Hope Seth

PROVIDENCE HOUSE PUBLISHERS
an imprint of
Providence Publishing Corporation
238 Seaboard Lane • Franklin, Tennessee 37067
www.providence-publishing.com
800-321-5692

Contents

ACKNOWLEDGMENTS   vii

FOREWORD   ix

Attitude   1

Change & Growth   9

Character   14

Compassion & Unity   26

Faith, Hope, & Joy   35

Family   45

God & You   55

Holidays & Seasons   68

Life Lessons   77

New Beginnings   87

Peace   92

Perseverance   96

Possibilities   104

Purpose   109

Relationships   115

Success & Work   127

Values & Truths   138

Wisdom & Prudence   142

Acknowledgments

I'd like to first thank my dentist, Dr. Jack Fletcher, for proposing this book while he had both hands in my mouth. He is one of many over the years who have suggested these radio spots should be put into print. Jack, however, did more than suggest. He went to work turning the dream into a reality. My thanks to a great host of friends who helped fund this adventure. You have been there for me through the years and I am grateful.

I would like to thank my administrative assistant, Carla Barrios, and her predecessors Joan Embry and Lois Baber who first organized my scribbling thoughts into some form and order. I would like to thank the people of Trinity Hill, St. Paul, and Brentwood United Methodist Churches who purchased air time where these *Faith Breaks* were first heard. The deadlines were a needed discipline.

I would like to thank Maxie Dunnam for his encouraging words. His friendship has been an inspiration. I would like to thank Nancy Wise, Andy Miller, and the people at Providence Publishing for their expertise.

Finally, I would like to thank my wife, Sandy, and our sons, Wes and Brad, who have increased my faith through the years and insisted that I take breaks which have often restored my soul. Above all, I am thankful to God for the gift of life and the opportunity to serve people. To Him be honor and glory forever!

Foreword

J. Howard Olds is among an elite group of gifted preachers who can communicate passionately and directly the transforming power offered in Jesus Christ. Throughout his remarkable ministry, Howard has demonstrated profound leadership, spiritual insight, and visionary pastoral administration.

I have been privileged to be closely associated with Howard during the years I have served as president of Asbury Theological Seminary in Kentucky. Before accepting the leadership of Brentwood United Methodist Church in Tennessee, Howard served outstanding churches in Lexington and Louisville, Kentucky. He was frequently elected to the General and Jurisdictional Conference delegations, where we served together, seeking to impact the larger church with the Wesleyan truth that we both share with such passion. He led our Kentucky delegation to General Conference in 2000.

I have journeyed with him through his painful struggle with cancer and have been inspired by the enormous faith and great strength he and his family have shown in his ongoing battle. Howard lives the truth that we all know, that the victory is in Jesus Christ the transformer and healer.

The writings in this small volume reflect the creativity and energy Howard projects in serving the body of Christ. Having originated as television and radio spots, they are light and uplifting reflections offered to the larger community of persons in and outside the church. I personally know the value of this sort of evangelism, as I offered a similar outreach during my ministry in Memphis, Tennessee. Many people have testified to the touch of these encouraging messages. They represent the mandate of Christ's great commission, creatively expressed in an appropriate manner to reach secular culture.

Howard's gift for expressing Christ's love for all persons is well articulated in the brief selections in this book. I know they will inspire everyone who reads them, and I commend the simple yet profound truths contained in these writings. They are a beautiful expression of the faith that all persons need.

Maxie D. Dunnam, President
Asbury Theological Seminary

Attitude

ATMOSPHERE

An astronaut was asked by a reporter to name the key to successful space travel. Without batting an eye the astronaut replied, "The secret to traveling in space is to take your own atmosphere with you." I've found that true for travels on earth, too. How about you?

The air in some rooms is filled with negative criticism. Breathe enough of it into your soul and you will become critical, too. Fill a meeting with talk of despair, and pretty soon the most positive people feel the doom of gloom. As my wise English teacher used to say, "Some people are just born in the objective case." Whatever the subject, they are against it. Given such attitude pollution, people are wise to take their own atmosphere with them. Such people provide a breath of hope in a room of despair, a positive note in a climate of criticism, a reason to move on against the objections of the day.

The next time you feel the effects of attitude pollution, do what the astronauts do—take your own atmosphere with you.

Grant us, O Lord, the power to be positive
in every circumstance, that we may bring
honor and glory to your name. Amen.

1

BAD IMPRESSION

A frustrated woman was making a scene on a city bus. She was rude, crude, and full of abusive language. As the woman was getting off the bus, the driver said, "Ma'am, you left something behind."

"What is it?" asked the woman scowling. "What did I leave behind?"

"A very bad impression," said the bus driver as he closed the door and drove on.

Whether we want to or not, all of us leave something of ourselves behind every day. What impressions are you making through your associations today? At work, at home, on the street corner, and at the traffic light, are you sowing seeds of kindness or spreading a spirit of strife?

Frustrations are sort of like mosquito bites. The more you scratch them, the more they bleed. Untouched mosquito bites disappear in twenty-four hours; scratched ones last for weeks. So in spite of our temptations to do otherwise, we would be wise to leave our frustrations alone. They heal quicker that way.

Dear Lord, since we never get a second chance
to make a first impression, grant us the grace to
do it right the first time. Amen.

BOREDOM

Believe it or not, I saw a spectator yawning at a football game the other day. The fans were loud. The cheers were roaring. This person found the whole thing boring.

For a moment I was relieved that people yawn in places other than church. Come to think of it, people can be bored just about anywhere. You can yawn your way through the Grand Canyon or sleep through a sunset. There were doubtless those who nodded off during Napoleon's coronation or Lincoln's brief Gettysburg Address. To be bored is to turn off whatever life is tuning in at the moment.

How about it? Are you bored to death? If so, it may say more about you than about the situations you are enduring. Boredom is more a state of mind than a set of circumstances.

So look around you. Find something of joy. Stay alert through life, for living is a thing we do, now or never. Which do you?

Thank you, God, for creating
a breathtaking world.
Keep us alert to the beauty around us
and the eternity within us,
that we may tiptoe through each day
as people with great expectation. Amen.

ENEMIES

A vindictive lady sharply criticized Abe Lincoln for his conciliatory policies toward the South. "After all," insisted the lady, "these are your enemies."

Lincoln, whose attitude often exceeded those of his time, replied, "But Ma'am, do I not get rid of my enemies when I make them my friends?"

Of course, Mr. Lincoln was right. The surest way to destroy enemies is to turn them into friends. People who care enough to hate usually have feelings strong enough to love. Critical people can become supportive people through the power of personal relationships. A little shift of attitude can make a world of difference.

The next time you are criticized or abused, walk a mile in your critic's shoes. Try to understand the situation from his or her perspective. Listen to the concerns. Instead of putting people in their place, try to place them in their best light. The change could make all the difference.

Merciful God, forgive us our hatreds
as we seek to forgive those who hate us,
in the sure and certain hope
you can transform a world of enemies
into a community of friends. Amen.

REVENGE

When it comes to the hurts of your life, do you try to get even or do you try to get over them? There's an old Greek legend about an Olympic athlete who begrudged the public acclaim given to the victorious competitor. His anger intensified when a statue was erected to honor the new champion. The sore loser vowed to seek revenge. Each night he secretly chiseled away at the statue's foundation. With each clash of the hammer, he dreamed of the day the statue would topple down. Sure enough, he succeeded. One night the statue fell and killed the man with chisel in hand.

Of this I am certain: Anger, jealousy, envy, bitterness, and hatred hurt us. They rob our peace of mind and destroy our physical health. People who seek revenge should dig two graves. One for the enemy. One for themselves.

Teach us, dear Lord, to leave vengence up to you,
that we may be free to live in joy and peace,
not merely survive in anger and hatred. Amen.

SAVING A STARFISH

As an old man walked the beach at dawn, he noticed a boy ahead of him picking up starfish and flinging them into the sea. "What are you doing?" inquired the man.

"Saving the fish," replied the boy. "Stranded starfish will die in the sun. I'm pitching the fish back in the sea. I'm saving their lives."

The old man glanced down the beach and said, "But the beach goes on for miles and miles and there are millions of starfish. How can your effort make any difference?"

The boy looked at the starfish he held in his hand. Then, throwing it back in the sea, he replied, "It makes a difference to this one."

No one can do everything, but everyone can do something. Let not the size of the problem spoil our determination of will. We may not be able to solve world hunger, but we can take a homeless person to lunch. We may not have the power to restore the environment, but we can clean up the mess in our own backyards. That makes all the difference.

Loving Savior, we realize we cannot
do everything to save the world,
so help us grasp the opportunities
at our fingertips to be like you. Amen.

WHY ME?

In a Tom Wilson cartoon, Ziggy says, "Whenever I ask, 'Why Me?' a voice always says, 'so who else did you have in mind?'"

Since morning never wore to evening without some heart breaking, a heart just as sensitive as yours or mine, most of us have played the Why Me? game. Why do bad things happen to good people? Why do tornadoes strike the just and unjust? Why, in the name of higher mathematics, do I become a statistic of disease?

When I sink into that quagmire of self-pity, I find it's time to change the question. I begin asking not "Why me?" but "Why not me?" Why do good things happen to bad people? How come it rains on the unjust as well as the just? Why should my disease be curable when another is terminal? Exactly who else should get what I have?

In the risky riddles of life, I've come to this conclusion: It's not what happens to us, but what we do with what happens to us that makes all the difference.

There are many things, loving God,
that our small minds cannot comprehend.
So help us trust you where we cannot see,
as we walk with you where we have not been,
guided by your omnipotent hand. Amen.

WORDS

Words, words, words, words, the world is full of words. Some words are big. Supercalifragilisticexpialidocious still sounds quite precocious. Other words are small, like "if." "If you can keep your head when all about you are losing theirs and blaming it on you."

Words can hurt. Remember that old saying, "Sticks and stones can break our bones but words can never hurt us." Don't believe it. Words do hurt. The cutting words of childhood still sting in the lives of many adults. Slinging mud in a war of words always causes one to lose ground. More damage is done in a moment of anger than this world realizes. Words do hurt.

Words can help. Words fitly spoken are like golden apples in a silver basket. The right word spoken at the right time, in the right way, in the right spirit, can change the world.

What words will you use today? Will they help or hinder? Will they build others up or tear them down? What about the words you will speak tonight? Will they break bones or build character? Encourage or discourage? Hurt or heal? Why not let them be wonderful words of life?

You alone, gracious God, have the
wonderful words of life.
Give us the wisdom to put our souls
in touch with you before we put
our mouths in motion about others. Amen.

Change
& Growth

ALMOST

In a "Peanuts" cartoon, Linus reviews the year's statistics of his baseball team. "In twelve games, we *almost* scored a run. In nine games, the other team was *almost* shut out. In right field, Lucy *almost* caught three balls. And once, she *almost* made the right play. WE LED THE LEAGUE IN 'ALMOSTS.'"

In the major league of life, do you ever feel that way? Life is seldom clear cut, black and white, all this and never that. Instead, life is a series of *almost, close, nearly, not far*. We *nearly* got the things we missed. We *almost* missed the things we got. Close plays in baseball are nothing compared to the *close* calls in life.

Maybe you are *almost* persuaded to be a better person, *nearly* convinced to live a better life, *not far* from choosing a finer focus. Why not turn your *almost* into *altogether* and go for it?

In the nearlies and not fars of our own lives,
O God, help us become altogether surrendered
to your will and your way. Amen.

HURRY UP

Hurry up! Have you already said that to yourself this morning? In our speedy, fast-paced world we are constantly telling ourselves and others that faster is better. We need to trade in our old computers because the newer ones are faster. Shopping is easier because it is constantly more convenient. Bewitched by this neurotic demand for things to be faster, quicker, and easier, we become incredibly impatient people. We even hurry up so we can slow down.

When will we learn that all things take time? Precious stones are not whipped out overnight. Solid character is not synonymous with instant success. Growth is not measured in milliseconds. Matters like integrity and relationships take time, usually a lot of time.

Frances De Sales once said, "Have patience with all things, but first of all with yourself." God makes all things beautiful in His time. If God is not in a hurry, maybe we would be smart to slow down too.

Slow me down, Lord, lest I run past more
than I catch up with in the rush of life
and miss the reason for living. Amen.

GROWING

Henry Wadsworth Longfellow brightened the world with encouraging words. This nineteenth-century writer experienced two great sorrows in the midst of his success. His first wife died quite young. His second wife was fatally burned in an accident.

An admirer asked Longfellow at seventy-five how he could write so beautifully and live so vigorously in the face of tragedy and old age? Longfellow, pointing to an apple tree that was a riot of colorful bloom said, "That is a very old apple tree, but the blossoms this year seem more beautiful than ever before. That old tree grows a little new wood each year, and I suppose it is out of the new wood that these blossoms come. Like the apple tree, I try to grow a little new wood each year."

Are you still growing? Whatever your age or sorrow, are you anticipating tomorrow? Why not try something new today. Bloom where you are planted.

Gentle Creator, keep creating in me a new heart,
that I may never grow weary of things as they
are, since you are making all things into what
they were meant to be. Amen.

Growth

REPAIRS AVAILABLE

A clock repair shop displayed this sign in the window: "If your *grandfather* needs oiling and adjusting, we still make house calls." As a grandfather, there are times I could use some *oiling* and *adjusting*. How about you?

The oil of *forgiveness* reduces *friction*. The oil of *understanding* eliminates hurt. The oil of *love* keeps us together. The oil of *joy* keeps us ticking. The oil of *hope* encourages us to try one more time. People need oiling.

People need *adjusting*. The demands of the day and pressures of the years can alter life's rhythm to the extent that we still tick, but not on time. We have not maintained the balance of work and rest, power and purpose, time and eternity. Major adjustments are needed to our timing.

If you could use some oiling and adjusting, remember that the Master Designer of the universe still makes house calls.

Bathe me, O Lord, in the oil of forgiveness,
that my soul may not grow tired and squeaky
through the seasons of life. Amen.

LESSONS FROM A TRAPEZE

They fly through the air with the greatest of ease, those daring performers on the flying trapeze. Nothing is more exciting at a circus than aerial acts of courage and grace. The pros make it look so easy. Of course, we know it's not.

According to those who know, there are two important principles that every high-wire performer must know. One is to let go. Those who fly through the air must first have the courage to turn loose. There is no way to grasp a new bar with your knuckles firmly fastened to an old one.

Many of us would like a better life, a new adventure, and a finer future. Have we the courage to turn loose of old securities in order to soar through the air toward a new dream?

The second ingredient of a successful aerial act is that of surrender. The flyer who tries to catch himself is certain to fall. So the flyer must wait for the strong arms of the catcher to bring him to safety.

Waiting with confidence may be our greatest challenge.

When I surrender my all to you,
dear God, remind me you will hold me tight
through the tides of time
until I am safe at last with you. Amen.

Character

GOODNESS

Do all the good you can, by all the means you can, in all the ways you can, to all the people you can, as long as you ever can—that was the motto of John Wesley, a mighty good man. When it comes to being good and doing good, how do you measure up?

Deep in every healthy person's heart simmers a longing to be a good person, at least a pretty good person. Our urge to be good must outlast other take-over bids of feeling good, making good, or looking good. Goodness is first and foremost a matter of being. If our hearts are right and our motives pure, then doing good becomes the natural fruit of those deep roots.

So when life is done and sun is setting, and it's all too soon a race that's run, how about it? Will people look at your remains in the casket and say, "There lies a good person"?

Lord, I would like to be a good person.
Purify my motives and guide my actions, that I
may become by your grace what I want to be
in my best intentions. Amen.

AUDIENCE

Reporters once asked baseball star Joe DiMaggio how he played so well so regularly. DiMaggio replied, "I always think there is at least one person in the stands who has never seen me play. I don't want to let that person down."

In the big game of life, who's your audience? Who are the people you dare not let down? There are colleagues counting on you. There are customers waiting for you. There are families depending on you. Day in and day out, there are good reasons to do your best no matter what.

I know pressure can be a problem, dailiness can do us in, routines can feel like ruts. All of us have days when we would just as soon stay in the dugout. That's when we need to remember there may be someone in the stands of our lives who will judge the game by the way we play it.

*Make us aware, dear God, that we
do not live alone. Others are watching us.
What we do, how we act, and the attitudes we
convey not only affect us but influence others
as well. So let us tread carefully, that we do not
fall and take others down with us. Amen.*

CHARACTER

Somebody said character is a lot like a window glass. Even a little crack shows all the way through. Character is the total of many small daily decisions. It is built on what we stand for, not what we fall for. It is the one accomplishment produced in this life that we can take with us to the next life.

Don't be a character; develop character—a steadiness of purpose, a clearness of vision, a singleness of spirit that helps you evaluate the immediate benefit in the light of the long-term investment.

A landlord struggles with rental policies. An author makes a decision about plagiarism; a researcher is tempted to alter data. A salesperson pads an expense account; a mechanic stands behind his work. Decisions like this make us or break us every day, for even a little crack in character shows all the way through.

You have not called me to be a character,
gracious God, you have offered to form my
character in your image. Give me the courage to
take you up on your offer, that I may be on earth
what I hope to be in heaven. Amen.

COMMITMENT

When it comes to commitments, how are you at making them and keeping them? Life's most famous fibs surely include these: I'll start my diet tomorrow. Let's have lunch sometime. We service what we sell. Your table will be ready in a few minutes.

Wanting to do more and be more than we are, we wind up promising more than we can produce. Good intentions that never get implemented compromise character more than we admit.

Some people handle the commitment challenge by never making them. They live like butterflies, moving from person to person, taking what they want without the slightest thought of the consequences. Where will we be in this world if the best we can expect from anyone else is, "I might be there, but don't count on it!"?

The key to commitment is realism. If we are careful not to make promises we cannot keep, we should be able to keep the promises we make.

Every promise you have made is mine,
dear God, for you keep your word. May the
promises I make to you and others be as laced
with integrity as your promises to me. Amen

CHEATING

Madison Sarratt taught freshman math for many years at Vanderbilt University. The wise professor had a favorite statement he always made the day students faced their first exam. "Today," explained Sarratt, "I'm going to give you two examinations; one in trigonometry and one in honesty. I hope you pass both. But if you fail one, fail trigonometry."

There are many good people in the world who cannot pass an examination in trigonometry. But there need not be a single person on earth who fails an examination in honesty. Honesty is essential for the survival of society. We must practice it in business, in families, and yes, even in schools. Honesty is not just the best policy; it's the only policy that pays in the long run. Did you pass the honesty test today?

We are tempted daily to cut corners and cheat others, all with the excuse that "everybody's doing it." Do not let us get by with such lies, searching God. Hold us to the standard of your commandments, that we may become your obedient children. Amen.

HONESTY

Honesty is the best policy. Apparently, however, fewer people believe that these days. According to a newspaper report, $100 billion in federal taxes go unpaid each year. Two out of every three high school students admit cheating on tests, some with the help of teachers. Forty-six percent of teenagers think lying is okay. Shoplifting is a multi-billion dollar business.

Honesty! Is it really too much to speak the truth in love? Is it really unreasonable to take only what you pay for? Has competition eroded character on the ladder of success? I suspect something happens to all of us when some of us choose dishonesty. A house built on half-truths, convenient lies, cut corners, and expedient cover-ups is bound to crumble. From the White House to our house, in the halls of Congress and the halls of high schools, we will do well to affirm honesty as the best policy!

You urge us to be truthful in our innermost
being, loving God. Help us to be honest with
you that we may learn to be honest with others.
And help us start right now! Amen.

INTEGRITY

Somebody said, "Integrity is a little bit like the weather; everybody talks about it, but nobody knows what to do about it." As America tries to recover from financial scandals in business and sex scandals in the church, we would do well to recover the lost art of personal and public integrity.

Integrity is about being a certain kind of person. It is about holding our lives together in such a way that we are the same inside and out, backward and forward, day in and day out. Integrity is not an optional accessory. It is a fundamental necessity for human survival.

Do you speak the truth, the whole truth, and nothing but the truth so help you God? Are you as honest in private as you are expected to be in public? Is your word as good as gold, your life as pure as silver?

Integrity is not about some victory won; it is the accumulation of days in which honorable actions are done.

Day by day, dear Lord, help us be people of our word, that our words may carry some weight in the routines of life. Amen.

AT WHAT PRICE?

A wide receiver on a national football team faked a fumbled catch by hitting the ground, rolling over the ball, and jumping to his feet in celebration. With his back to the official, the player managed to fool the man in charge, even though a national television audience could clearly see the truth. The television commentator exclaimed, "What a head's up play," being loosely translated to mean, "Wow, what a great liar that kid is," as the team marched down the field.

Now, suppose that player had an unlikely surge of conscience causing him to approach the official saying, "I'm sorry, sir, but I did not catch the ball, your call was wrong." Such honesty would have likely left fans furious and his future contract in jeopardy.

And that raises another question! In America, has our need to win done in our desire for integrity? In the boardroom as well as the locker room, has competition caused us to camouflage the truth hoping all along we don't get caught?

Since your grace has made us all winners
with you, loving Savior, save us from
the temptation of trying to look better
before others than we really are,
that we may be more like you. Amen.

LIAR, LIAR

In the movie, *Liar, Liar*, school children are asked to identify their parents' professions. "My mom's a doctor," says one little boy. "My dad's a truck driver," chimes in another. But Max says, "My dad's a liar." What follows is a teasing, touching story about one father's struggle to keep his word with his son. The antics of actor Jim Carrey are absolutely funny. The struggle for honesty, especially with our children, is absolutely real.

What are the promises you've failed to keep with your children? "We'll get together sometime." "We'll build the tree house later." "I'll call before bedtime." The list is endless. Pretty soon our actions speak louder than our words and our children sense the inconsistency.

In the movie, Max makes a birthday wish. His dad, Fletcher, is then forced to speak the truth. The results are chaotic and converting. But finally, Fletcher comes home to himself and his son. What will it take to restore your integrity with your sons and daughters?

Our Father in heaven, since we dare to call you
parent, help us be the kind of parents that will
not destroy our children's faith in you.
Help us be trustworthy, that they may come
to trust you, living lives of integrity
as you have called us all to do. Amen.

EMERGENCIES

A skydiver jumped from an airplane and pulled the ripcord, but nothing happened. Remembering his emergency chute, the diver pulled the ripcord again. Nothing happened. Looking fearfully toward earth, the skydiver spotted a man flying upward from the earth. As the two passed in midair, the skydiver shouted to the other man. "Hey, buddy, do you know anything about parachutes?"

The guy going up shouted back, "No, do you know anything about gas stoves?"

Emergencies prove to be poor times to seek instruction. Yet, it seems half the world is seeking advice from the other half while both sides are sitting in the same darkness. That's why we need eternal answers to everlasting problems. Resurrection stares death in the face and promises hope. A present God promises never to leave us nor forsake us. And the world will work if you are willing to do unto others as you would have them do unto you.

A person is what he or she proves to be in an emergency.

O Lord, since you are on call all the time,
let us never hesitate to seek your help
during the emergencies of our lives,
so we may dwell with you in safety. Amen.

CROOKS

"You just can't trust anyone anymore!" Do you embrace that belief?

Steven Brill decided to challenge that theory in New York City. Brill went undercover as a well-to-do foreigner with little knowledge of English. He got into several dozen taxi cabs to see how many drivers would cheat him. What do think happened? Only one driver out of thirty-seven did him in. The rest took him directly to his destination and charged him correctly. Several refused to take him when his destination was only a block away. Some even got out of their cabs to give him directions. Most warned him to be careful for New York City was full of crooks.

Trust is an ultimate value that protects civilized society from chaos. Maybe people are more honest, trustworthy, respectable, and responsible than we think. At least I hope so. And as for me, I can determine to be so.

Red and yellow, black and white,
all are precious in your sight. Loving Jesus, give
us eyes to see others as you see them,
that we may live by faith, not fear. Amen.

TRUST

Lucy, in a "Peanuts" cartoon, is deploring her lack of trust in people. She explains to Linus that she trusts him only as far as he can throw his blanket. With that, Linus tosses his blanket as far as he can pitch it. Later, Linus explains to Charlie Brown, "Lucy trusts me exactly eight feet."

How far do you trust the people around you? Shakespeare advised us to "love all but trust few." Trust is not automatic anymore; maybe it never was. It takes time to trust. Yet, trust between a husband and wife, a parent and child, an employer and employee, a business and its customer, a government and its people, is absolutely essential to effective society. People who cannot trust anybody anymore are locked in a prison of loneliness and ineffectiveness.

Let us be trustworthy people. Let us keep our promises and maintain our integrity. Let us be dependable, reliable, and responsible, so people will be able to trust us further than they can throw us.

When I surrender my all to you, dear God,
remind me you will hold me tight
through the tides of time
until I am safe at last with you. Amen.

Compassion
& Unity

FACES

Have you heard the old story about President Thomas Jefferson and a group of companions riding cross-country on horseback? The presidential entourage came to a stream swollen by spring rains. There by the water's edge stood another traveler hoping for a lift to the other side.

As the president and company passed, the traveler approached Jefferson for a ride. The president took the man on his horse and set him down on the other side.

A presidential aide challenged the traveler. "Why, sir, did you approach the president of the United States for a personal favor?"

"I didn't know who he was," confessed the traveler. "I just know some faces say, 'no' and some faces say, 'yes.' His was a 'yes' face."

On the daily highways of life, do we project a "yes" face or a "no" face? Are we courteous, caring, and concerned, or critical, calloused, and cold? Our faces may reveal more than we think.

May the expressions of our faces, precious Lord,
reveal a heart that has been blessed and
redeemed by your unconditional love. Amen.

WHY DIDN'T YOU COME?

On the second day of school a kindergartner approached his teacher and said, "Why didn't you come?" Not knowing what the child meant, the caring teacher asked him to explain. "Why didn't you come when my mother died?" said the boy.

"I didn't know your mother died," replied the teacher. "I am sorry. How did it happen?"

"Everybody knew," insisted the boy. "It was on television. My daddy choked my mamma to death. Why didn't you come?"

This true story haunts me every time I tell it. God has placed in the hearts of little children the instinctive knowledge that some things are not right. Children know they should not suffer alone. Every time I see another abuse or abduction in the news, I think of that little boy. Maybe it's because his question cuts across the barriers of race, class, and religion. Compassion knows no east or west, no north or south. It longs for one great fellowship of all the human race. Suffering people, whatever their age, rightly ask, "Why didn't you come?"

*Gracious Lord, give us the courage to act
on our convictions and bring comfort
to some child who is suffering alone
and wondering why. Amen.*

DEMONIZING

As our homes are pounded daily with political ads, I find myself beginning to wonder, "Why are we so intent on demonizing those different from us?" We live in a time when "birds of a feather flock together" and find security in squawking at others. It evidently gets election results. It obviously produces sponsors for talk shows. But, let's be reasonable for a moment. Is life so neatly divided into good guys and bad guys, right beliefs and wrong beliefs, us and them?

There is an old jingle that goes like this: "There is so much bad in the best of us and much good in the worst of us, that it hardly behooves the rest of us, to be critical toward any of us." People who are content to sling mud may gain dirt in political polls but lose ground in the cause for civil communities.

How about you? In public and in private, do you speak the truth in such a way that those affected by it feel loved?

Forgiving Savior,
when fear drives us to shut people out,
grant us the grace we need to draw new circles
that take people into the human family
of mutual concern. Amen.

VISION

Will Rogers once said, "It don't take much insight to see that something is wrong, but it takes some real eyesight to see what will make it right again."

Vision is a picture of our preferred future. Without vision, people perish. Yes, problems are real. Certainly critical analysis is essential. Problems need to be defined but not dwelled upon. It's one thing to curse the darkness. It's quite another thing to light a candle.

How will you spend your energy today? Cutting people down or lifting people up? Cursing or creating? Resisting or revolutionizing? Vacillating or visioning?

The world will seldom remember the things we oppose. All creation could benefit from the visions we support, provided we have the determination to let our dreams shape our destiny.

Let us become a kinder, gentler, more loving and caring society. Let it begin with me.

Bold Creator, you have told us
that people without a vision perish.
Give us your visionary Spirit, we pray,
that we may find creative possibilities
in what seems like chaos. Amen.

COMMUNITY ON
AN ELEVATOR

Once upon a time, I got stuck in an elevator for nearly two hours. In close communion with twenty people, I witnessed the ways of humans in an emergency. Some panicked; others prayed. Some grew silent; others became verbal. Some waited; others went to work dismantling anything that could be taken apart. A clear unity emerged among the group driven by the common cause of getting out quickly and safely. Black and white, young and old, women and children, fathers and grandfathers pulled together. There were no divisions nor dissensions in our common quest for fresh air.

While this community of people will never assemble again, I have reflected much on our common experience. If people can come together in times of emergency, why can't we pull together for the good of society? If we can lay our differences down in a quest to escape, why can't we set our differences aside for the sake of freedom? If we can become a community in an emergency, is there not hope for community all the time?

Gracious God, you have made us
for community but we choose to live in our own
self-centeredness. Bring us out of our caves of
hiding, that we may work together
for the good of humanity. Amen.

THE GOOD
SAMARITAN NEARBY

Researchers at Princeton Theological Seminary asked forty ministerial students to walk next door and give an impromptu speech on the Good Samaritan. Meanwhile, researchers planted a slumped, groaning, broken man beside the sidewalk on which the students had to travel. Guess what! More than half the ministerial students passed by the broken man without stopping.

So, the age-old story of stopping to help somebody is still true. While people bleed beside the road, most of us are content to read about it, talk about it, maybe even attend conferences concerning it. Meanwhile, thank God for the minority who walk the walk, not just talk the talk. They have eyes to see, ears to hear, hearts to care, and resources to share. They take time to stop, time to listen, time to help the best they can.

In our desire to do good, let us be careful not to pass by the true meaning of compassion.

If we are going to talk the talk of concern,
dear Lord, give us the heart to
walk the walk of compassion. Amen.

GUERRILLA GOODNESS

Guerrilla goodness! I ran into that phrase the other day, and the more I use it, the more I like it. In guerrilla warfare, troops who fight behind the lines in occupied territories keep on fighting when others have surrendered. Guerrilla soldiers are tough, determined, dedicated, focused. They have a mission and no one can stop them.

What if we applied that principle to peace, not war? What if a small band of people decided to make every city a better, safer, fairer place to live? What if a group of people started practicing random acts of kindness and senseless deeds of beauty with determination? What if ordinary people in ordinary neighborhoods started protecting streets, loving neighbors, watching out for each other, and caring for the lonely?

Guerrilla goodness. Its time has come. The government can help. Schools play a part. Social systems provide vital service. But no institution can take the place of a single person determined to make the world a better place.

Merciful Savior, help me practice
guerrilla goodness in the trenches of my daily life,
that the world may be a better place
for all who pass by. Amen.

THE LIFE OF A CHILD

A hundred years from now it will not matter what my bank account was, and no one will remember the kind of car I drove. By then, my dream home could well be bulldozed down in the name of progress. But, the world may be different because I was important in the life of a child.

As schools open their doors once more, let us open our hearts to life's most precious gift—our children. Let us resolve, as good citizens, to improve the quality of education whatever the cost. Let us team with teachers to make our schools places of hospitality and hope. Let us personally engage in the lives of children, those we call our own and those who have no home.

Have you hugged your kid today? Have you volunteered to help some child find the way? Can you temper your greed enough to see the child in need? Can you find the time to listen to the little one in line?

Someday it won't matter how much we make nor how many things we leave behind. But, I can make a difference by touching the life of a child.

Loving Jesus, we remember that you gathered the children in your arms and blessed them. In the rush and fury of our daily lives, give us the compassion to follow your example. Amen.

DOING
YOUR OWN THING

Jewish author Elie Wiesel tells the parable about a man in a boat. The man is not alone, although he acts as if he were. One night without warning, the man decides to cut a hole under his seat. Other people on board are alarmed. "What on earth are you doing?" they exclaim. "You are going to destroy us all!"

"Why are you alarmed?" replies the man. "What I am doing is none of your business. I paid my fare. I am not cutting under your seat. Leave me alone."

Wiesel concluded his parable with this comment: "What a fanatic will not accept but you and I cannot forget is that we are all in the same boat."

We are all in the same boat. Whether or not it is clear to us, we are not free to do our own thing as long as the thing we do affects our fellow passengers. Survival in the boat of humanity depends on cooperation, consideration, community. Remember that the next time you are tempted to start sawing under your seat.

Dear God and parent of us all,
make us aware of our traveling companions
on the boat of life and keep us from
doing things to please ourselves
that may bring harm to others. Amen.

Faith, Hope, & Joy

THE CROSS

A strange cross hangs in a small town church. It is neither brass nor polished wood. It is simply two old roots tied together. Yet around that crude cross people gather from the community to remember, rejoice, and pray.

One spring raging waters tore that town apart. Factories flooded. Homes were destroyed. Schools washed away. People gathered to save the little community church. They built a barricade. But, the dike sprung a leak, and people ran for higher ground—except for one man. He managed to edge a tree across the leak. Debris filled the hole. Later, he cut two roots from that old tree, tied them in the form of a cross, and hung it in the church—a symbol of victory over despair.

The cross at which Christians bow to worship was rugged, too. But this emblem of suffering and shame became a sign of hope and joy. With God's help, we, too, can rise again.

Let the cross upon which you died,
dear Jesus, be a constant reminder
that you redeem the worst that can happen,
giving us the grace to rise again. Amen.

KEEPING ON KEEPING ON

A letter to Ann Landers went like this: "I am an eighty-six-year-old woman who is still keeping house, driving my car, and enjoying life. I was blessed with a wonderful husband. He lived to celebrate sixty-one years of marriage with me. This morning I decided to do some washing. I put my clothes in the machine, patted the side of the washer and said, 'Do your job, baby.' It did. While watching television, I thought, 'Dear God, what a wonderful life I lead.' I am not wealthy, but I'm not poor, either. I am just a simple, average, middle-class old lady who is living on Social Security and feeling truly blessed. Signed, Mary"!

Could you write a letter like that? Has the joy of life touched your heart yet? I know, you have work to do, burdens to bear, problems to solve, life to manage. Each day seems like a mountain—a mountain too steep to climb. Successful mountain climbers learn to enjoy the trip as well as anticipate the summit.

Keep alive in me, O God, the joy of living,
that I may embrace each day
as a special gift from you. Amen.

Joy

BIRTH AND DEATH

What's it like to die? In my profession, it's a constant question. Since I haven't "been there and done that," I really don't know what it's like to die. People in near-death experiences describe bright lights, floating feelings, and inner peace. At best, death is a mystery, a voyage into the unknown. What if death is something like birth? Who knew what it was like to be born? To leave the safety of a mother's body, where one is cushioned against hard knocks, connected to the source of nourishment, and has every need fulfilled, is a frightening journey indeed. Even our first welcome to this world includes back slapping and mucus suctioning. But something else awaits a newborn: loving parents, elated grandparents, hugs and kisses, joy and laughter, potential and possibility.

To take one leap and learn you are immortal is more than my small mind can imagine. Yet by faith, I embrace it all the time.

From you we come and to you we shall return,
merciful God. Help us make that journey
in the sure and certain hope that
you will meet us on the other side. Amen.

THE DOOR

I buried my father the other day. At eighty-eight, he had lived a full life and was more than ready to move on to a new realm of being. His last request was for help to get through the door, a door we have come to believe symbolizes everlasting life.

Some say death is a danger, an endless aching threat. And death can be fearful. Some say death is an ending, a loss of all that is. Death is a loss of presence. For time, like an ever-rolling stream, bears all who breathe away.

But I say death is an entrance, a door into eternal life. When day by day we walk with God and find the assurance that we are His own, the summons to leave this life is at best an invitation home. Beyond the horizon of our known world, there is so much more life to be lived, joy to be shared, wisdom to be learned. Whatever you do, find the door that leads to life.

Dear Jesus, you are the door to everlasting life.
Give us the grace to enter that door
like people who are finally home from
a very long trip. Amen.

ICE CREAM CONE

Life is kind of like an ice cream cone. The moment you think you've got it licked, it drips on you.

We are forever trying to get life under control, once and for all. We plot. We plan. We search. We save. We work. We wonder. Will a bad economy rob us of retirement? Will divorce drive our children back home? Will company downsizing do us in? Will illness or even death take our life away? Somebody said, "The problem with life is that it has an 'if' right in the middle of it." So it does.

Will we let the drips destroy the joy? Anxiety steal excitement? Problems rob us of possibilities? I hope not.

Ice cream can be good, drips and all. One of life's greatest sights is still a child enjoying an ice cream cone. So keep on licking. Life is worth it.

Let us taste and see that you are good,
dear Master, so we may live life licking,
not feeling licked. Amen.

GENEROSITY

Oseóla McCarty, a Mississippi washer woman, had to drop out of school in the sixth grade. She celebrated her long life, however, by giving the University of Mississippi $150,000 for scholarships. She never got an education, but she wanted others to have one. People asked Oseóla why she didn't spend all that money on herself. She smiled and said, "Thanks to the good Lord, I did."

What is life's greatest joy? Is it getting or giving? Is it having or serving? Is it collecting or contributing? The generous people of the world want for others what they never had for themselves. They rejoice at the success of others without envy or jealousy within themselves. They are free to give what they have so others may get what they need. Some know no reason to be born, save to consume the corn, eat the fish, and leave behind a dirty dish. And then there's Oseóla McCarty!

Teach us, wise God, to put in more than
we take out, that we may leave the world
a better place than we found it. Amen.

GOLF

The golf pro was giving his sixth and final lesson to a slow learning student. "Your main problem is that you stand too close to the ball," lamented the instructor, "after you swing."

I've been in that predicament, haven't you? Not just on the fairways of a golf course but on the fairways of life, too. We get all set up and give life our best swing only to discover that we are not far from where we started. Bad habits are hard to break. Poor stances cause us to slice life, as well as golf balls.

As sure as there is a right way to hit a golf ball, there is a right way to live a life. If you are tired of swinging harder and getting nowhere, maybe it's time to consult a pro. God likes life; he invented it. He can teach us to play life's game with joy and fulfillment.

Teach us, masterful Lord,
to play the game of life as winners,
lest we wind up alone feeling like losers. Amen.

GOD KNOWS YOUR NAME

In a Tom Wilson cartoon, Ziggy is visiting his psychiatrist. "It started out with the post office," laments Ziggy as he reclines on the couch. "Now everybody calls me occupant."

Day by day, you and I are depersonalized in multiple ways. Somebody published this little piece in the *Wall Street Journal*:

> *My social security number is easy,*
> *My banking number I can spout,*
> *Phone numbers and zips are always ready,*
> *But my age I have to figure out.*

In addition to being numbered, we are constantly categorized. We are employers or employees, parents or children, boomers or busters, black or white. We are Protestant or Catholic, Methodist or Baptist, Christian or Jew. People become more predictable when we can put them in their place.

While institutions want to number us and people like to pigeonhole us, God still calls us by name. The Lord of the universe knows when I sit down and when I rise up. God knows me personally and cares for me eternally. And that makes all the difference.

> *You call us by name, O Lord.*
> *Let us never take that personal relationship for*
> *granted as we seek to know your name. Amen.*

SMILE

A smile is the light in the window of your face that lets people know your heart is at home. Did you get that?

A smile costs nothing but creates much. It enriches those who receive, without impoverishing those who give. It happens in a flash, but its memory lasts a lifetime. Smiles create happiness in the home, goodwill at the office, and encouragement on the street corner. It is rest to the weary, uplifting to the discouraged, and sunshine to the sad. A smile is nature's best antidote to trouble.

And let there be no doubt about it. A smile is more than an upward curl of the mouth. Smiles start in the heart. They are the outward and visible signs of an internal peace. When the heart gets right, the face is sure to follow.

Joyful God, you give us good tidings of great joy.
May our hearts remind our faces that we have
great reason to rejoice in you. Amen.

SOUL LIFTS

Maxwell Maltz is a plastic surgeon. He has spent his life changing people's faces. Dr. Maltz says, "Even though I get marvelous results, patients are often not happy. I have come to realize that inner scars are much more difficult to remove than outer ones."

Could your soul use a lift today? Is there some inner scar that won't go away? Life can leave us beaten and battered. Over the years, a hurt here and a heartache there, a trouble then and a turmoil now, can take its toll on our souls. Pretty soon it requires more than a face-lift to improve our self-image. Respect, self-esteem, compassion, and freedom are new looks that require surgery on the inner most parts of our being.

That can happen for you. There is a Great Physician who is in the soul-lifting business. Why not let the love of God give you an inner lift? It could change your life.

Good Shepherd, we thank you
for restoring our souls. Keep leading us
in paths of righteousness for your name's sake,
that we may dwell in your house forever. Amen.

Family

THROUGH THE YEARS

Tom and Mary Lou, who were celebrating their sixtieth wedding anniversary, were asked by a reporter how they did it, given that so many marriages end in divorce these days. Tom thought a moment, then said with a smile, "Well, every day I tell Mary Lou how much I love her and every week I tell her something new that I appreciate about her. After forty years of doing this, she came to believe I was the most insightful man that ever lived."

Are you still in love with the one you married, and do you find fresh new ways to express your admiration? I stood beside a casket as another man said good-bye to his childhood sweetheart. They, too, had been married for sixty years. Through his tears he said, "I love her now more than ever and I long to hold her once more in my arms." Through the years, love grows deep and strong. Through the years, two become one. Are you keeping love alive through the years?

Lord, you keep your commitments to us.
Teach us to keep our commitments
to one another, that we may grow in love
through the years. Amen.

THE PRACTICE OF
APPRECIATION

What do you like most about your spouse-to-be? I've learned over the years to ask that question of every couple who comes to me to be married. I've gotten some interesting answers. "She's good looking." "He's my best friend." "She's a shoulder to lean on." "He respects me as a person." The list goes on. It's not the list but the habit that makes a difference in married life. It's hard to fight with a marriage partner who tells you every day that you're great and wonderful.

This practice of appreciation applies to other family members, too. Have you told your children lately that you love them? How about a little game for your family's dining pleasure tonight? Go around the table and let each person complete the sentence, "What I appreciate most about you is . . ." then really listen for the answer. Watch love grow.

Life can beat us, defeat us, and leave us feeling low. That's why we need a family to restore our souls.

When you created us, O Lord, you rejoiced
that your accomplishment was very good.
Help us appreciate one another
as much as you appreciate us. Amen.

ACCEPTANCE
AND ACCOUNTABILITY

Parenting is one of life's primary responsibilities. While there is no sure-proof guide for raising responsible kids, here are a few hints that I have found helpful in parenting my own sons.

1. Love your children unconditionally. Never make acceptance an "iffy" matter.
2. Make a clear distinction between "helping out" and "taking over." Assist, but never too much.
3. Treat failure as a necessary part of success. Above all, avoid name-calling for goofing up.
4. Evaluate accomplishment according to ability. Eliminate comparisons and be cautious about competition.
5. Encourage personal responsibility for actions taken. Blame is a destructive game.

Shaping a life is serious business. The world's most important decisions are not being made in the White House but in your house. In the day-to-day routine of parenting, we are producing the people who will shape society for the twenty-first century. May God help us do it well.

Heavenly Parent, you have entrusted us with the awesome responsibility of raising your sons and daughters. Give us wisdom to do it well, that our children will grow up to joyfully call you Father. Amen.

IN SPITE
OF EVERYTHING

A couple decided to celebrate their fortieth wedding anniversary with a quiet evening for two. After a nice dinner, the wife picked up a champagne glass, looked lovingly into her husband's eyes, and began her toast with these words: "In spite of everything." Maybe that wife was right on target.

Love, in the long run, is more endurance than excitement, more decision than delight, more commitment than infatuation. Love at first sight is easy to understand. It's when two people have been looking at each other for forty years that love becomes a miracle. If we can know each other's faults and failures, experience each other's weaknesses and worries, endure each other's obsessions and obligations, and in spite of everything, still offer a toast of respect and admiration, we may finally know the nature of real love. True love endures all things, believes all things, hopes all things. True love never ends.

You never promised us a rose garden, dear Lord,
you simply asked us to keep tending the garden.
So when it comes to family, keep us digging
for love in all the right places. Amen.

MUTUAL ADMIRATION
SOCIETY

Mutual Admiration Society—does that describe your family? An old proverb suggests, "Pleasant words are like a honeycomb, sweet to the soul and health to the bones." Healthy families are mutual admiration societies, where people are appreciated and praised. Big problems seldom tear families apart. It's the dailiness that drains us—the slow erosion of closeness that leaves us strangers in the night.

Is your home a refuge from the noisy rattle of the world? It can be. People come home to be picked up not beat up, appreciated not apprehended, at peace not at war. We who inhabit our homes can make them havens of rest and places of peace. We can practice random acts of kindness and participate in the pleasing game of interchanging praise.

Look right around you. Find people in need. Praise a family member today. As Mark Twain put it, "I can live two months on a good compliment."

Help us, loving God, to believe in others
as much as you believe in us.
And grant us the grace to tell them so. Amen.

LOVE

There's an old British proverb which states, "Faults are thick where love is thin!" Have you found that to be true? Love covers a multitude of sins. Where love abounds problems become possibilities, differences are diminished, doubts are cast away. Love dreams, delights, persists, forgives, and, yes, even overlooks.

Are not two people in love at the marriage altar the same two people who stand before the judge in divorce court? What changed? Personalities are probably the same. Issues are usually constant. People are people. The difference is the love factor.

"What's love got to do with it?" screams Tina Turner in a popular song. "Who needs a heart when a heart can be broken?" If love produces patience and kindness . . . if love bears all things, believes all things, endures all things . . . if love lasts . . . the question is not who needs it, but who can possibly relate without it? Faults get thick when love runs thin.

Eternal God, you are love and you love us with
an everlasting love. Open our hearts to receive
your love, that we may be able to
love one another as you love us. Amen.

PARENTING

If you want your children to keep their feet on the ground, put some responsibility on their shoulders. Have you considered that?

Most parents want good things for their children. Many of us would like our sons and daughters to have it better than we had it growing up. So we provide more, give more, go more, hoping our children will have the very best of everything. Good parents need to give their children good gifts.

However, here's the question. In our giving, are we contributing to their growing? Maturity implies responsibility. If we help our children become accountable in small things, they will learn to be responsible in many things. If we allow our children space to work out their small problems, they will develop the art of solving major problems.

Effective parents provide both support and space, both acceptance and accountability. You can't have one without the other.

In the close quarters of family life, dear Lord,
give us your grace that we may be good
role models for our children and treat them as
mercifully and justly as you treat us. Amen.

HANDLE WITH CARE

Somebody stamped an important reminder on a package I received the other day. In bright red letters it said, "Fragile, Handle with Care." Actually the contents were not that expensive, just a photo of my family sandwiched between two flats of cardboard. The message, however, was priceless.

Are you handling your family with care? In the close quarters of family life the worst side of ourselves is well known. Tempers flare. Words fly. Feelings are hurt. People break. It would be a happy day in most relationships if we merely treated our families with the same courtesy we extend to strangers. Love and respect, patience and understanding, communication and consideration, that's what good homes are made of. People are precious and often fragile. Let us handle each other with care.

You know how fragile we are, precious Lord,
easily broken, quickly distracted.
Mend the cracked places of our souls,
that we may be filled with your love until
it overflows to others. Amen.

ROOTS AND WINGS

As teenagers pack for college and kindergartners prepare for school, thoughtful parents wonder if their children are equipped for what's before them. In times like these, I slip back to an old saying which seems to say it all: "A set of roots and a pair of wings, have you given your children these two things?"

Both college students and kindergartners need roots and wings. Deep roots steady us in the storm. Deep roots find water in dry places. And wings are necessary for life. However hesitant parents may be to let their youngsters out the door, we know our offspring must be pushed from the nest if they are ever going to fly. To clip their wings is to cripple them for life. We must let them go.

With a set of roots and a pair of wings, our children can explore the unknown without being disowned. They can feel the brilliance of the breeze without sacrificing the groundedness which keeps them going.

Lord of earth and sky, you give us roots
and invite us to spread our wings.
May we encourage our children the way
you inspire us, holding us gently yet freely,
inviting us to fly. Amen.

WEDDING

The bride was really nervous on her wedding day. So, her father offered this advice as they waited arm-in-arm at the back of the church. When we start down the aisle, concentrate on the aisle. You've walked this aisle before. As we move toward the altar, think about the altar. People meet God at church altars. God will meet you. Then when we near the front, look into the eyes of your husband-to-be. Think about him. Concentrate on the joy you are about to share. The bride grew calm. The wedding went smoothly—except some guests on the ends of the pews wondered why the bride kept whispering, "aisle altar him; aisle altar him," all the way through the processional.

Few marriages make it when either spouse decides to alter the other. It takes acceptance and affirmation to build a relationship. We are not perfect, but it never helps to have a spouse who tells you so.

How about your marriage? Is it sinking in a sea of criticism or growing in the ground of love?

*Since you are the only master human beings will
ever need, grant us, gracious Lord, the power to
join our hands in love for one another
as we bend our knees in devotion to you. Amen.*

G o d
& Y o u

A Q U A R I U M

Author Philip Yancey reflects on the aquarium that adorns his office, making these human observations from the fish that dwell therein. "To those fish, I am deity. I balance the salts and trace elements in their water. No food enters their tank unless I put it there. The fish would not live a day without the electrical gadget that supplies oxygen. I fight off the parasites, bacteria and fungi that invade their tank.

"You would think my fish would adore me, and be deeply grateful. Not so! Every time my shadow appears above the tank, they dive for cover. I am too large for them, too incomprehensible, my acts of mercy they see as cruelty."

How do we humans respond to our Provider? All we have needed, God's hand has provided. Morning by morning new mercies we see. Night after night God's grace is sufficient. Are we grateful? Do appreciation and praise shape our days? Is worship a part of our lives?

Help us not to be afraid of your power,
mighty God. May all our running be
toward you not away from you.
Keep us in your protective care. Amen.

ENERGY

As I was playing golf recently, I found myself on the back side of the course, far away from the clubhouse, in a cart with a dead battery. It had enough power to get me out there, but not enough energy to bring me home. I was stuck, stranded, stopped, delayed.

A friend of mine used to say, "I go to church to get my batteries charged." We need spiritual energy to navigate the hills and valleys of life. We need divine power to find our way home. We need wisdom from on high to make it here below.

If you have run out of energy on some hill far from home, if you are weary in well doing or maybe too tired to roam, then it's time to renew your inward energy and find the power from on high to travel wisely here on earth.

Why not find a place to worship this week? Join a community of faith who will keep you connected with God. It may be time to recharge your spiritual batteries.

When we in our own strength confide,
our striving will be losing.
So come beside us, mighty God, with the power
of your own choosing.
Make us adequate to the tasks that you
set before us, that we will not falter
on the hills of life. Amen.

BRIEF IS BEST

Have you noticed that some of life's most important speeches are best known for their brief phrases? "The only thing we have to fear is fear itself," declared Franklin D. Roosevelt, to inspire a nation. "I shall return!" said General MacArthur. And who could forget those words of John F. Kennedy in his inaugural address? "Ask not what your country can do for you, ask what you can do for your country!"

Simply put, the principle is this: Brevity is usually best. That could be true of our prayers, too. There are brief prayers I try to pray every day. "Thank you, Jesus." "Help me, please." "Christ, have mercy." "Others, Lord, yes others." Such prayers take little time but have eternal significance. They calm the mind, focus the soul, warm the heart, and lift our eyes beyond the confusion of the moment.

Whisper a prayer this morning. Remember to pray at noon. Say a brief prayer in the evening. It will keep your heart in tune.

It's not our words but our wills that please you,
O Lord. So let our prayers be brief
and our lives be better. Amen.

FUNCTIONAL ATHEISTS

Functional atheists. I ran into that phrase the other day and I keep thinking about it. Specifically speaking, a functional atheist is a person who believes in God but continues to live as if God does not exist. Such persons are believers in theory, but atheists in practice. They acknowledge the existence of God but ignore the presence of God in daily life. As a functional atheist, I may be watched by God from a distance, but such awareness makes no difference in the decisions I make or the roads I take.

Is this a description of you? In reality most of us live our lives, pursue our dreams, raise our families, and do our jobs as if God does not exist. While an all-knowing, all-powerful, all-wise God waits in the wings, we spend our time on life's stage trying to remember our lines, avoid embarrassment, and be recognized by others. If only we knew what is eternally true—God is not leaving it all up to us. Our lives are in God's hands. Relax and believe.

*Lord, we confess that we live our lives as if
you do not exist. We try to do it ourselves when
you are there all the time, waiting patiently in
line ready to help if we will only ask.
Now we are asking. Amen.*

PRAYER FOR THE DAY

Consider offering this prayer to get you through the day. "Lord, keep me from the habit of thinking I must say something on every subject under the sun. Release me from the craving to straighten out everybody's affairs. Keep me free from confusion and give me wings to get to the point. I ask for grace enough to listen to the tales of others' pains and patience enough to endure my own.

"Teach me the glorious lesson that occasionally I may be mistaken, even downright wrong. Give me the ability to see good things in unexpected places and talents in unexpected people. And give me, O Lord, the grace to tell them so.

"Make me thoughtful but not moody, helpful but not bossy, patient and not pouting. Give me a little something to forgive each day that I may grow in understanding of your unlimited forgiveness of me. And may I walk softly and tread gently around the lives of all your children, making today count and anxiety about tomorrow cease."

With a prayer like that in the depths of your heart, you can make every day a good day.

Prayer puts all things in perspective, dear Lord,
so we come to you in prayer.
Make us and mold us after your will
while we are waiting, yielded and still. Amen.

LINCOLN

He was seven years old when his family was forced to move from Kentucky because they couldn't pay their bills. At nine his mother died. At twenty-two he lost his job as a store clerk. The woman he dated four years refused to marry him. He lost more public elections than he ever won. He had a nervous breakdown. His four-year-old son died. At fifty-one he was elected president. In his second term he was assassinated. As Lincoln himself put it, "I often go to my knees because I have no place else to go."

Where do you go when adversity strikes? To rage, to drink, to sex, to depression? Trouble can dump you into the quicksand of despair or deliver you into the hands of a loving God. If your knees are shaking, try kneeling on them.

After all, it was integrity through adversity that enabled Lincoln to say: "When I have lost every other friend on earth, I shall at least have one friend left. And that friend shall be down inside me."

When we fall on our knees before you, loving God, we are introduced to power beyond ourselves. So lift us by your might, that we may overcome the troubles we've seen and find strength and help in time of need. Amen.

LONELINESS

In a Tom Wilson cartoon, Ziggy is talking on the phone. "I don't really care about the time and temperature," laments Ziggy, "I just called because I'm lonely."

Loneliness. It may be one of the most universal sources of suffering today. The child feels it when classmates laugh at him. The teenager feels it when she is excluded from the dance. Even many parties and friendly get-togethers leave us empty and sad. In a frenzy to fake it, we surround ourselves with noise, get lost in the crowd, and even use the phone to dull the pain.

What if we could turn loneliness into solitude? What if we stayed in the valley of loneliness long enough to see the flowers bloom? What if we really could walk through the shadows and discover divine company? The saints of history did not handle loneliness by running to the noise. They handled loneliness by placing their hands in the hand of the One who calms our fears, even in the valley.

We are never alone, precious Lord, when you
are near. Help us find you in the valleys and
walk with you through the shadows,
that our souls may be restored
and our hearts comforted. Amen.

PERSPECTIVE

Abraham Lincoln once said, "I can see how a person might look down on the earth and be an atheist. But I cannot conceive how anybody could look up into the heavens and say there is no God."

Lincoln was right. Perspective does make all the difference. We can get so engulfed with the hell on earth that we become blinded to the beauty of heaven. Dealing with problems all day long leaves us believing life is just one difficulty after another.

If your in-look has dimmed your out-look, maybe it's time to consider an up-look. Behold the heavens, the moon and stars which God put in place. Remember that same Creator has you on his mind, your good at the center of his will, your well-being at the core of his heart.

Gallop polls tell us 94 percent of Americans believe in God, but only about 23 percent of us believe God to be a friend. God is watching us, not just from a distance, but right here in the thick and thin of our daily lives.

Lord, we need to feel your presence
as well as know your existence. We are not
alone, we live in your world. Give us that
perspective as we live each day. Amen.

IN GOD WE TRUST

I found a penny on a sidewalk the other day. Perhaps it was dropped through a hole in someone's pocket and passed over by others who thought it was not worth picking up. After all, what's a penny worth these days? Bubble gum costs a nickel. Given inflation, it is hard to get half your two cents worth with a penny anymore.

However, as I rubbed the dirt from my new discovery, I found a message worth more than money can buy. Inscribed on our coins, even pennies, are these words: In God we trust.

In God we trust. We will be wise as a nation to take this conviction placed on our currency by our forefathers and mothers and inscribe it on our hearts as well. Trust in God can break down the walls that divide us. Trust in God can save us from weak resignation to the evils we deplore. Trust in God can remind us there is more to making a life than simply making a living. Trust in God can unite us, lift us, and make us a kinder, gentler nation.

What we inscribe on our coins, O Lord,
let us write on our hearts. Let us trust in you
and not be afraid. For you make everything
valuable in your time. Amen.

A BETTER WAY
TO PRAY

Have you left your home today? Did you think to pray? Sooner or later, sometime or another, nearly everyone prays. Some people pray regularly. Others pray occasionally. Some know God as an intimate friend. Others shout at him as they would a stranger. Of course, God is big enough to listen to all kinds of prayer.

There are, however, effective and ineffective ways to pray. It is one thing to make God an errand boy. It is quite a different matter to crown him Lord. Most of our prayers sound like grocery lists. We pray for God to bless our plans while we live our lives as we please. "Lord bless us, our children, our friends, our family, our jobs, and our joys. Amen." All of us pray like that now and then.

There is a better way to pray. Instead of asking God to bless us, why not invite God to make us a blessing? "Dear God, give me eyes to see, ears to hear, and feet to follow your will in the world, that I may be a small part of the great things you are about to do today."

Now that is a powerful way to pray. Try it, you might find it helpful.

Lord, whatever you are doing today,
I would like to be a part of it.
Give me the honor of working for your kingdom
instead of trying to build my own kingdom.
Let my desires be pleasing in your sight. Amen.

JUMPING TO CONCLUSIONS

A psychologist, an engineer, and a theologian were on a hunting trip when they came upon an isolated cabin. They knocked, but no one answered. The door was unlocked, so they went in. Immediately they saw a large, pot-bellied stove suspended in midair by wires attached to the ceiling. The curious site stimulated speculation. The psychologist said, "This lonely trapper has elevated his stove so he can curl up under it and vicariously experience a return to his mother's womb."

The engineer had another idea. "This man is practicing the laws of thermodynamics. He's discovered a way to distribute the heat evenly throughout the cabin."

The theologian had a loftier idea. "Fire lifted up has been a religious symbol for centuries."

As the argument heated up, the trapper returned and gave this simple explanation: "Had plenty of wire, not much stove pipe."

By the way, what false assumptions have you made lately because you failed to consult the Creator?

Since things are not always what they seem to
be, help us, gracious God, to consult with you
before we draw conclusions on our own.
For we are wiser and smarter when we do. Amen.

STAY ON YOUR KNEES

A mountain climber's greatest desire was to climb the Matterhorn. Finally, he saved enough money, hired the best guide, and climbed his way to the top. The winds were fierce, but the view was breathtaking. As the climber started to rise from his knees to celebrate his victory, the wise old guide yanked him back and screamed in his ear, "Stay on your knees, man, or the wind will blow you off the mountain."

This solid principle of mountain climbing could well be true of life, too. People walking through the valleys of the shadow are prone to pray. They have nowhere else to go. While prayers are important in the valley, they are essential at the summit. People on top of things have the farthest to fall. People at the summit are the most vulnerable to subversiveness. It's risky at the top. Have your knees bent in gratitude and prayer lately?

Lest we slip and fall we stay on our knees before you,
wonderful Savior. Keep us humble and
able to listen to your small voice.
Should we reach the mountain top,
make us anxious to give you all
the honor and glory. Amen.

WORSHIP

President Franklin Roosevelt often attended a particular Washington church. The people of that congregation tried to be courteous with sightseers who came to worship for the sole purpose of seeing the president. One Friday afternoon the pastor answered the phone and the caller on the line inquired, "Tell me, do you expect the president to be in church this Sunday?"

Patiently the pastor replied, "I can't promise that the president will be here this Sunday. But we do expect God to be here. We think that's reason enough to attend."

If you are attending church to check out the crowd, you might do better at a party. If you are attending church for the performance, you will do better at the center for the arts. If business contacts are your concern, I recommend civic clubs. But, if you want to meet God, find forgiveness for your sins, direction for your life, and spiritual company for your journey, then church is the right place to be. Come join us.

In worship, loving God, we acknowledge you
to be worthy of our love and praise.
Help us now to worship you. You are Lord,
you are king, you are our everything. We bring
all glory and honor to your name. Amen.

Holidays & Seasons

NEW YEAR

"Let's walk to the horizon and see what's beyond it," says the bird to the turtle in a "B.C." cartoon.

"Nothing doing!" replies the turtle. "I walked to the horizon once to see what was beyond it and all I found was another Horizon."

Here on the horizon of a brand new year, we may discover life to be much the same. There is work to do, bills to pay, problems to solve, life to live. As one person put it, "Life is just one darn thing after another." So it is.

Somewhere in the shadows of our own souls, we decide. We decide to face tomorrow with hope, courage, and adventure. Or, we set out to endure tomorrow in despair, desperation, and discouragement. Why not make a New Year's resolution that could really make a difference? Decide now to face each moment and live each moment with faith, hope, and love. Make every tomorrow an adventure. You'll be glad you did!

At the dawn of a new year, O Lord,
we offer ourselves to you.
May this year be an adventure in your presence
with new horizons of meaning and hope.
Fill us with your Spirit, that we may follow you
and not be afraid. Amen.

SPRING

I'm ready for spring. Let the rain stop and the sun shine. Let the mud settle and the flowers bloom. Let the fish bite and the gardens grow. Yes, I'm even anxious to crank up the lawn mower.

Every time I experience earth's coming-out party, I stand amazed at the power of resurrection inherent in nature. Natalie A. Sleeth put it this way in her song, "Hymn of Promise":

> In the bulb, there is a flower.
> In the seed, an apple tree.
> In cocoons, a hidden treasure:
> Butterflies will soon be free.
> In the cold and snow of winter
> There's a spring that waits to be,
> Unrevealed until its season,
> Something God alone can see.

Even greater than new life on earth is new life in us. We can rise again. We can grow. We can add a measure of beauty to the earth. We can make our world a happier, holier place to live.

Grant us new life in the depths of our souls,
dear Lord. Let us grow into your likeness,
that we may do your work on earth
as it is done in heaven. Amen.

CUT FLOWERS

As spring once more unwraps the flowers and we behold earth's growing powers, I'm reminded of the observation that "ours is a cut-flower generation." We enjoy the benefits and beauty of life, but we no longer have a source of nurture outside ourselves.

Cut flowers beautify our tables, enhance our worship, even make strong statements of love and concern. Who does not delight in a pick-me-up bouquet? But, cut flowers never last long. They wilt, dry up, get discarded. The memory may continue, but the flowers are gone.

On the other hand, flowers with roots keep returning. They may lie dormant all winter, but they bloom in the spring. Many bloom not once, not twice, but all summer long.

Are you a cut-flower person or a deep-rooted person? You can be connected to the water of life, rooted in the soil of relationships, nurtured by the nutrients of faithfulness, and bloom where you are planted for a lifetime.

Let us be rooted in you, good Lord, that we may
be empowered to bloom where we are planted
not for just a season but for all eternity. Amen.

SIGHTSEEING

As summer vacations come into full swing, I wonder if we know the difference between looking and seeing? A man stepped into the Cathedral of Notre Dame hoping to experience the God of the ages through the sights and smells of this grand sanctuary. As he settled down into quiet meditation and prayer, a bus load of tourists stormed into the place. They scurried through the cathedral pushing past people, racing from corner to corner trying to get a perfect picture in the limited time allowed by the tour host. On the way out, one man said to his wife, "Was that the Cathedral of Notre Dame?" With an affirmation from her, the man proudly made a big check mark on his sightseeing check list.

There is a vast difference between looking and seeing. Beholding the beauty of the earth may be much different from seeing the sights of some selected vacation spot. No wonder we return from vacations more exhausted than when we left.

Give us eyes to see, dear Lord, what is in plain view. Help us not to run past more than we catch up with. Let us see the beauty of creation, the accomplishments of civilization, and the wonders of the universe with new eyes and new appreciation. Amen.

Seasons

HALLOWEEN

Is it my imagination or is Halloween becoming a major American holiday? This annual parade of ghosts, goblins, witches, and fear seems to get bigger every year. While I have no desire to be a ghostbuster, sometimes I wonder what is behind our fascination with the underworld? Is it merely mass marketing? Is satanic music to blame? Or do witches and devils so live inside us that once a year we have to express what most of us no longer believe? The reformer, Martin Luther, put it this way: "Though this world with devils filled, should threaten to undo us, we will not fear for God has willed His truth to triumph through us."

So, let us have Halloween. Pretending is fun. But let us find our heroes, not in the ghosts of the night, but in the saints of the day, who knew how to fight with evil and win.

Help us, eternal God, not to be fascinated with devils, but delight in the saints who have persevered in the past and found the courage to carry on. Let us rejoice in the light of shining martyrs who gave their lives that we might live and know how to love. Amen.

DECEMBER

Here we are in December. December is not so much another month as another state of mind. People do strange things in December. They bring trees inside their houses and light up their yards like living rooms. They fill their calendars with festivities and then complain about being too busy. People go more, spend more, entertain more, and eat more in December than any other time of the year. How can something so wonderful leave us so weary?

Here are some suggestions for making December more delightful and less demanding:

1. Take a little time for quiet meditation. Let your soul catch up with your body.
2. Don't expect too much. Difficult family members will continue to be difficult in December.
3. Choose your activities wisely. Hectic paces produce hostile people.
4. Live within your means. The most valuable present you can give is your presence.

Slow me down, Lord. I do too much, go too often,
and push too hard—especially in December.
Give me the space to walk upon a midnight clear
and hear the angels sing, that my soul
may be restored for the holidays. Amen.

Seasons

MIRACLES

"Do you believe in miracles?" inquired the young adult as he exited a worship service. When I answered affirmatively, the young man sighed deeply. "Good," he said. "I sure need one." As I pondered that brief conversation, I thought of Walt Whitman who walked through ordinary days recording notes on the wonder of life. Miracles to Whitman were not unusual, extraordinary events. He had eyes to see miracles on the streets of New York, in the waves of the ocean, beside the grass of an open field. Miracles for Whitman were not beyond nature but in nature—like the exquisite delicate thin curve of a new moon.

December delights us with make-believe. It's larger than life, newer than normal, busier than usual. But, miracles are more than make-believe. While Bethlehem bars bustled with festivity and government officials calculated the population, a tiny bare-bottomed baby was born that changed the course of the world. Let us who need a miracle stop long enough to look.

We marvel at the miracle of your birth,
merciful Jesus. Give us eyes to see and hearts big
enough to imagine all you had in mind for us
when you came to earth. May the miracle of
Christmas fill us with hope and joy. Amen.

SAVIOR OR SANTA

In a Hank Ketchum cartoon, Dennis the Menace sits on Santa's lap, making this lament, "Do you have any idea how hard it is for me to be a good boy all year long?" When it comes to being good all the time I can empathize with Dennis. How about you?

That's why the real meaning of Christmas has more to do with a Savior than a Santa. "You better watch out, you better not pout, you better not cry, I'm tellin' you why; Santa Claus is coming to town." Meanwhile, we do pout, we do cry, and we do fail to watch out.

As the silent night of Christmas nears, let us affirm once more the eternal truth that Christ the Savior is born. A savior does for us what we cannot do for ourselves. A savior picks us up, pulls us out, breathes into us the breath of life. It was precisely because we couldn't get it right that Christ the Savior was born.

Since it is hard for us to be good all the time,
we depend on you, loving Savior, for forgiveness
and new life. You alone can pick us up when we
are down, so we depend on you
for what we cannot do for ourselves. Amen.

Seasons

MISGIVINGS

Now that Christmas is over, the reality of our hit-or-miss generosity sets in. Streets and shopping malls are packed today with people trying to give back what they didn't want in exchange for something they believe they need. The sweater didn't fit. The tie didn't match. The tool didn't work. The toy wouldn't run.

All misgivings are not of the material kind. Relationships get mixed up, too. Childhood pain runs deeper than we imagine. Manipulation feels confining even when camouflaged in fine gifts. Hurt feelings fail to be automatically resolved. Christmas leaves us with our misgivings.

What can we do? We can be honest with ourselves and others. We can bring our shattered dreams and wounded hearts into God's storehouse of love. We can exchange guilt for grace, rejection for acceptance, despair for hope. We can pick up the pieces of our lives and move on, with neither shame nor neglect.

When life is hurtful, forgiving God,
help us not to give up.
Instead, let us bring our misgivings to you,
that you may mold and make us new. Amen.

Life Lessons

CONFIDENCE

Someone described confidence as something you have before you understand the real situation. Picture this image: an elegantly dressed woman, at a sophisticated social occasion, is holding a cup of coffee. Her little finger is placed ever so daintily, and her face reveals complete self-assurance. Unfortunately, she has no idea that her slip is collapsed around her feet. Confidence is something you have before you understand the real situation.

Or to put it another way: things are not always what they seem. From a distance, people appear to be manageable and problems should be solvable. From a distance, relationships ought to work and peace prevail. From a distance, marriage is easy, parenting is fun, and work is a piece of cake. Life, however, is not lived from a distance. Life is lived up close and personal. On the slippery slopes of complicated, often confusing circumstances, we feel our way along, one step at a time.

Lead us, Lord, one step at a time, that we may gain the confidence to walk with you all the days of our lives. Fill us with your love, that we may live hopeful lives, confident that your grace is sufficient for every need. Amen.

CONSUMERS

Do people consume to live or live to consume? Ah, that is the question for modern Americans. In 1976, the average supermarket carried nine thousand products. Today the same supermarket will carry thirty thousand products. With a good antenna, homes in the 1950s could get three television stations. Now, with three hundred stations available, people still complain there is nothing to watch. What is this insatiable appetite for more that is delivered to each person daily by thirty-five hundred ads seen and heard? Have we redefined the essence of being into "I shop, therefore I am"? Has marketing become so effective that things we didn't even want yesterday become absolute necessities today? Do we have things or do things have us?

I like things. The conveniences of today make the "good old days" not so hot. I do, however, think it's time we used things instead of allowing things to use us. Purpose and meaning are matters of soul, not selling. Wise is the person who knows the difference.

*Consume us, merciful God, that we may not
be consumed by the things that surround us.
Set our hearts on things eternal, so all things
material may find their rightful place.
Make us more like you. Amen.*

COMMITMENT

Glynn Wolfe died in 1977 at the age of eighty-eight. That name is probably not familiar to you, but according to the *Guinness Book of World Records*, Glynn Wolfe married more times than anyone else in the world. Twenty-nine times altogether, Glynn promised a woman that he would love, honor, and cherish her forever. I wonder if bride number twenty-nine had trouble taking Glynn at his word?

Commitment! How can we build a trustworthy world without it? If the best we can expect out of one another is a tentative agreement to hang around as long as you meet my needs, feed my ego, and pamper my narcissism, what kind of homes can we build for our children? No wonder the number one fear of kids is that their parents will get a divorce.

Certainly there are times when divorce is the best alternative for a bad situation. I sense, however, that many divorces are matters of convenience, resulting from lack of commitment.

Lord, remind us that you are completely
committed to us so that we
can commit ourselves to one another.
Help us be dependable and faithful
in all our relationships, that we may live
as you would have us live. Amen.

LIFE GOES ON

Life goes on. "Those three words," wrote Robert Frost, "sum up everything I have learned about life." Life does go on. Without our help the sun rises on another day and the stars continue to shine in the night. Even when circumstances cause us to scream, "Stop the world, I want to get off," life has its way of going on. Consistently and persistently, when it seems too long or feels too short, when it seems all right or even feels wrong—life goes on.

And you know what? I'm glad it does. I'm glad the sun does not depend upon my moods nor the days upon my efforts. I'm glad the times and the seasons are in God's hands and out of mine. I'm glad we can only predict the weather not produce the weather. Put the weather at the disposal of human endeavor, and anarchy would surely follow.

So, take comfort in this sure and specific certainty. Life goes on.

Our lives are in your hands, loving God, and we
can trust you to help us carry on. Give us faith
to walk where we cannot see
and courage to trust our lives to thee.
For with you life goes on. Amen.

RUN AWAY

A policeman noticed a little boy riding his tricycle around and around a city block. The boy had a lost look on his face and a lot of stuff on his tricycle. So the officer stopped the boy and asked him where he was going.

"I'm running away from home," said the boy.

"Then why do you keep going around and around the block?" asked the policeman.

"Because my mother won't let me cross the street," said the boy.

I suppose children of all ages feel like running away sometimes. I know I do. Life gets too demanding, too stressful, too complicated to keep on keeping on. That's when I thank God for instilled messages of character and conscience that set safe boundaries for my need to get away. Such guides for life keep us safe on the sidewalk instead of reckless in the middle of the street.

Sometimes we feel like running away, dear Lord.
The pressure is too much, the demands are too
many. Hold us within the boundaries of your
grace, so that even when we wander
your gentle hand will keep us safe. Amen.

Lessons

SMALL STUFF

Have you noticed the big difference that can be made by a little attention? I know we often say, "Don't sweat the small stuff." It is possible to micromanage our way out of business. But, large differences often start through a little attention. Many years ago, a French physician watched some children playing. One child began tapping on a board with a small stone. At the other end of his plank, another child listened. The doctor continued to mull over the observation. Out of that reflection came the invention of the stethoscope, one of medicine's primary tools.

In most of life, it's the little things that count. Businesses rise or fall by the first impressions of customers concerning courtesy and helpfulness. Factories function best by paying attention to precise craftsmanship on the assembly line. Homes are knitted together by small deeds of kindness and thoughtful acts of respect and devotion. Yes, the small stuff does make a difference.

Creator God, you not only made things big, you made things small. In the tiniest cell there is life. Turn our attention, O Creator, to the small things of life, that we may learn your ways and walk in your will. Amen.

AFFLUENZA

Comedian George Carlin once said, "The essence of life is trying to find a place to put all your stuff!" How about it? Are you drowning in your own stuff? There are thirty-two thousand self storage businesses nationwide. Rubbermaid sells one hundred million storage containers a year. Professional organizers will come to your home, and for approximately seventy-five dollars an hour, organize your clutter. The successful person snaps his Midas fingers and people jump. Yet when a person seems to have it all, the castle comes crashing down, and everything he or she touches turns to garbage.

There is life beyond the American disease of affluenza. Maybe it's time for you to be set free from addiction to stuff. If all you've ever wanted is not enough, let the Lord of the universe pick you up, set you free, and give you an eternal reason to be.

Make us aware, loving God, that we are more than what we possess, greater than what we create. Give us eyes to see beyond the temporal, that we may be able to embrace the eternal. Fill us with a great reason to be. Amen.

TIMING

I was traveling down a busy highway when my car stopped, stalled, died, and wouldn't start. There I sat, stuck in the middle of rush hour traffic. I had the car towed, and a few days later the mechanic called to tell me the problem. "Your timing is off," he said. "That's why the car won't run."

If timing is urgent in sports, music, clocks, and cars, is it not likewise important in life? "To everything there is a season," said a wise person long ago. "A time for every activity under the sun." So there is a time to plant an idea in the mind of an inquisitive child, and a time to sow a seed of hope in the heart of someone hurting. There is a time to work and a time to wait. There is a time to rush and a time to rest. There is a time to play and a time to pray, a rhythm to every purpose under heaven. Attention to timing can keep us from stalling on the highways of life.

You make all things beautiful in your time,
precious Lord. Make us aware of your timing
and give us the grace to follow your lead,
lest we stall on the roads of life
and fall by the wayside. Amen.

TRAVELING

Summertime is vacation time for most families. It's been said vacations come in three stages—anticipation, participation, and recuperation. You are probably in one of those stages right now. Years ago, as our family pulled out of the driveway for summer vacation, one of my sons leaned over the backseat and said, "Dad, when we get to where we are going, where will we be?" It was a question I've dared to keep.

When you get to where you're going, where will you be? Over the years, I've discovered the real purpose of vacation is to restore the joy of being home. No hotel bed sleeps like my bed. No restaurant food tastes like home-cooked food. No roller coaster ride replaces my enjoyment of a lounge chair. The excitement of leaving is never as great as the joy of coming home.

Therein lies the secret of life. We are all trying to find our way home—home to a self we can live with, home to a God we can connect with, home to a family who won't let us go.

In all our going, gracious God, lead us gently home. We feel a need to explore the outer regions and experience the unusual. But what we need is eternal security and solid foundations. Help us know that our final rest is with you. Amen.

WAITING

In a lifetime, the average American will spend five years waiting in line, two years returning phone calls, eight months opening junk mail, and six months staring at traffic lights. In spite of modern technology, the first sign we often see on the computer screen is "please wait." Phone customers nowadays expect to be put on "hold."

Do you wait with purpose or perplexity? To wait or not to wait is not the question. The only question is how we wait. According to statistics, the cost of running red lights is seven billion dollars a year. The average time saved is fifty seconds. Traffic jams are seldom solved by the blowing of horns. Cursing does not seem to get customer representatives on the phone more quickly. However, kindness does dissolve wrath, and prayer is a good way to wait through long delays.

May you be present in the waiting moments
of our lives, good Lord, that we may wait
with purpose instead of frustration.
You hold our moments in your hand.
Help us live them in your presence. Amen.

New Beginnings

TODAY

As I watched a production of *The Music Man* recently, I was captured once again by Professor Harold Hill's one honest line in a series of bold lies to the people of River City, Iowa. You may remember Salesman Hill has fallen in love with Marian, the small town librarian. As Harold tries to persuade Marian to marry him without waiting, he says, "You pile up a lot of tomorrows and you'll find you have collected a lot of empty yesterdays."

Are you missing some present joy by wishing for some elusive tomorrow? When school starts, when the children are grown, when the promotion comes, when retirement arrives—it will be different then. Will it really be different then? If we miss present opportunities by always anticipating future chances, we may find we have collected a lot of empty yesterdays. Today is the first day of the rest of your life. Make the most of it.

We recognize today to be the day of salvation,
saving Lord, so help us not put off until
tomorrow what we need to do today.
Grant us the grace to live in the now,
seizing every opportunity to do your will
and follow your way. Amen.

GOOD INTENTIONS

Thanks to the Internet, somebody brings me a church bulletin blooper every week. One I recently received was from Corvallis, Oregon, where a lenten worship sermon was entitled, "The Safest Road to Hell" followed by this offer: "Transportation provided. Please call before noon Saturday."

"The road to hell is paved with good intentions," says an old proverb. Indeed it is. We don't need anybody to lead us into temptation; we are quite equipped to find it on our own. Every day we are confronted with little platitudes that, left unchallenged, will finally do us in. *I'll get around to it tomorrow. I can quit anytime I want to. I'm just human. Nobody's perfect. I meant well. The devil made me do it.*

A better life is not down the road of good intentions, but at the corner of decisive action. We cannot get to where we'd like to be by simply traveling faster in the wrong direction. Sometime we need to stop, turn around, and start over.

Lord, we intend to be better than we
sometimes are, but we need you to move us
beyond our good intentions. It takes decision
and concrete action to be your disciples,
so let us start walking in the direction
that you are leading. Amen.

I'M SORRY

In a Hank Ketchum cartoon, Dennis the Menace is saying his evening prayers. "I'm sorry," prays Dennis, "but I've got a whole bunch of 'I'm sorrys' for you tonight."

There are nights when I feel a lot like that. Life has its faults and failures. We do those things we shouldn't do, and neglect the things we need to do. That old prayer of confession has not changed for centuries.

But you know what? I've learned not to be sorry for being sorry. Confession is good for the soul. Love includes forgiveness. It takes a stronger person to face mistakes than to deny them. A brand new start is always possible.

The next time you face your God with a whole bunch of faults and failures, remember this: We need never be sorry for being sorry.

We confess our sins to you, redeeming Jesus,
in the sure and certain confidence that
you will forgive our sins and cleanse us from all
unrighteousness. So help us be sorry in a way
that will be beneficial to us and others. Amen.

ERASER

In a Hank Ketchum cartoon, Dennis the Menace is sitting in the corner being disciplined for drawing pictures on the living room walls. In his time of reflection on the damage done, Dennis comes to this conclusion: "I wish life came with an eraser."

Among life's greatest inventions, I can think of nothing better than an eraser on a pencil or the delete key on a word processor. I use them often. On the larger pages of life, we do those things that we ought not do. We make mistakes. Words are spoken that would be better left unsaid. Faulty people are bound to fail from time to time.

Forgiveness fits faulty people. Forgiveness is an eraser attached to the pencils of time. It is God's way of granting a clean slate and people's way of starting over.

Forgiving God, blot out our transgressions and
forgive our sins that we may have a clean slate
on the tablets of time. We err and stray from
your ways like lost sheep. In loving kindness,
come and find us. Amen.

SECOND HALF

A talented basketball team played a miserable first half. They shot poorly, defended badly, and generally failed to play as a team. By half time, they knew they were in deep trouble. They knew the coach would scream at them with good reason. Can you imagine their surprise when the coach didn't show up in the locker room? The players just sat there in silence. No one said a word. Each replayed his every mistake in his own mind. Then, just before the second half was to begin, the coach walked in and said in a single sentence the very thing they needed to win the game. "Gentlemen," said the coach, "you've got a great second half inside you."

There have been times I could have used that kind of coaching in the big game of life. It doesn't take a lot of insight to point out the mistakes we make. We feel the pain and suffer the consequences. What we need is someone to believe in us when we are having trouble believing in ourselves.

You never stop loving us, Lord,
so we find in you the grace we need to carry on.
We are blessed by your mercy and empowered
by your Spirit to do better in the future
than we have often done in the past.
Therein lies our hope. Amen.

Peace

SELF-SERVICE

Self-service only. The signs seem to be everywhere these days, at grocery stores and gas stations, in cafeterias and convenience shops. We are a "take what you want" kind of world. We have learned through the years to "fend for ourselves," "stand our ground," and "wait on no one." This is the American way of life.

Such aggressive consumerism affects our religion, too. People are more interested in what churches can do for them than what they can do for their churches. Most of us would rather do it ourselves than depend on God. After all, God's timeline seldom matches our scheduled lives. We are in a hurry. God takes eternity. Someone said God created humanity in his image, and we have been returning the favor ever since by trying to squeeze God into our likeness.

If you are tired of self-service, there is another way. Through surrender and community, we can find peace. Try it. You might like it.

We try too often, Lord, to do it ourselves.
We come to you as a last resort instead of a
first option. Forgive us, we pray. Help us find the
peace that passes all understanding
as we surrender all things to you. Amen.

CHOOSING YOUR
BATTLES

"You got to know when to hold 'em, know when to fold 'em, know when to walk away, and know when to run." There's something about those lyrics from that old Kenny Rogers' ballad that rings true to life. Day by day, in multiple ways, we decide the battles to face and the conflicts to avoid.

There are things worth fighting for. There are principles and values that deserve our defense and need our support. There is a time to take a strong stand and determine, whatever the cost, to do no other. But not always. Choose your battles wisely. Is it really worth the fuss to fume over which movie to watch tonight? Does a small scratch on your car really warrant a suit in small claims court? If kids insist on cutting across your yard, does the damage deserve a confrontation?

Certainly we must decide. But more and more I am deciding that some fights are just not worth winning, and the peace that passes understanding gives greater joy than all the commotion of a conflict.

Help us, Lord, to know when to speak up and
when to be silent. Make us truly wise that we
may do your will in all circumstances of life,
not seeking our own glory but only your will
in things that really matter. Amen.

PEACEMAKING

Lucy is chasing Charlie Brown in a "Peanuts" cartoon. "I'll catch you," shouts Lucy, "and when I do, I'm going to knock your block off!"

Suddenly, Charlie Brown screeches to a halt. He turns to Lucy and says, "Wait a minute, Lucy. If you and I as relatively small children, with relatively small problems, can't sit down and talk through our problems in a mature way, how can we expect the nations of the world to get along?"

With that, Lucy slugs him. "I had to hit him quick," she said. "He was beginning to make sense."

Of course, Charlie is absolutely right. Peacemaking begins in the intimacy of home and family. Parents are the real heads of state and ambassadors of peace. Abused children often grow up to be violent adults who produce more abused children. Somewhere the cycle must stop.

Let us resolve in little ways to quit quarreling so nations will no longer rise up against nations, and people will study war no more.

Prince of Peace, come dwell in our hearts,
we pray. Take all our hurts and fears away.
Bathe us in your love until we feel the need
to study war no more. Amen.

WAR AND PEACE

As the threat of terrorism and the talk of war wears on our minds and hearts each day, where do we find the strength to carry on?

We can try to ignore it. But it won't go away. We can even make jokes about it. But our laughter barely shields the face of fear. We may feel like succumbing to the anxiety but that would only paralyze us permanently.

So how do we go about our normal lives in the light of reality? Let me suggest some ways: Begin each day with a prayer for peace, including the personal peace that passes all understanding. Build community in your little corner of the world. We need one another. And in times of fear, we need one another even more. Worship regularly. We can worry about situations beyond our control or surrender our lives to the only one who knows what tomorrow may hold. At the center of this storm may you find a place of calm to help you carry on.

Wars and rumors of wars have become a way
of life, dear Lord. Where can we find peace?
Hold us close, that we may know security in an
insecure world and peace in a world prone to
hate. Guide our paths, that we may
dwell in safety today. Amen.

CURVE BALLS

Major league baseball batters must learn to hit curve balls. They likely prefer pitches thrown down the middle, but that seldom happens. It's curve balls, sinker balls, knuckle balls, high balls, and low balls coming across the plate. To make it in the majors, great batters must learn to hit whatever comes at them.

Life throws curves, too. If we had it our way, we'd ask for slow pitches and sure hits. Instead, unexpected curves cause us to strike out. While we can't control the pitcher, we can improve the batting.

The next time life throws you a curve, don't complain, "Unfair," to the Umpire in the sky. Hang in there. Practice, learn from strikeouts, study, listen. In time, you will discover a great truth. Curve balls can be hit for home runs, too.

You never promised life to be easy, gracious God;
you only promised that your grace would be
sufficient. May your grace be adequate to the
challenges we face today. Help us rise above our
own abilities as we place our trust in you. Amen.

ERRORS

In 1986, Bob Brenley was playing third base for the San Francisco Giants. In the fourth inning of a game with the Atlanta Braves, Brenley made an error on a routine grounder. Four batters later he kicked away another grounder, then threw wildly to home plate committing two more errors. A few minutes later Bob muffed another play to become the only major league player to make four errors in one inning.

Bob Brenley could have given up. But he didn't. In the bottom of the fifth, he hit a home run. In the bottom of the seventh, he hit a single driving in two runs to tie the game. In the bottom of the ninth, Bob Brenley hit a massive home run into the left field seats to win the game for the Giants.

Whether you are playing baseball or trying to make a hit in life, never let your errors get you down. Step up to the plate with confidence and become a winner.

Our lives are full of errors, O Lord.
We slip and fall, we miss the ball,
we make a multitude of mistakes.
Fill us with your grace. that we may get up
one more time than we fall down and
become winners in the big game of life. Amen.

PRACTICE MAKES PERFECT

Pablo Casals was one of the great cellists of all time. Even at age ninety, the master continued practicing the cello four to five hours a day. "Why, at your age, do you keep working the fundamentals?" inquired a friend.

Pablo Casals replied, "Because I think I'm making some progress."

All of us would do well to have that kind of determination way down in the depths of our souls. After all, life is a matter of making progress, at being what we are meant to be. Goodness and badness mingle in the veins of the best of us. People who faithfully practice the fundamentals of integrity and honesty, justice and mercy, and love and kindness are the truly great people of the world.

Let us never be overcome with evil. Rather, let us overcome evil with good. Day by day, for all our days, let us earnestly strive to be our best, nothing more, nothing less, nothing else.

Probing Master, let us never settle
for less than we can be.
Inspire us to push the limits of possibilities
you have placed within us.
Never let us grow weary in well doing. Rather,
let us strive for the best and nothing less. Amen.

DEAD OR ALIVE

A minister friend of mine was declared dead by the federal government, even though he is very much alive. Some type of bureaucratic mistake caused the problem. His bank account was frozen. His Medicare payments were discontinued. From a legal point of view, Jim was dead, and it took him several months to convince Social Security otherwise, even though they talked with him by phone. "It's not every day you can reach the dead by telephone," quipped Jim, who kept his sense of humor the entire time.

I wonder if there are other living things that we have somehow declared dead too soon? It's easy to declare a marriage dead at the first sign of difficulty. We give up on children before they have a chance to find themselves.

Signs of resurrection can be discovered in the most dormant circumstances. May this day bring you hope and help of a divine kind, and leave you yet alive.

You have the words of everlasting life,
dear Jesus, speak them into the dead places of our
hearts, that we may experience a resurrection.
We trust you to make all things new. Amen.

DETERMINATION

Every day this fatherless boy gazed at the fence separating his family's ramshackle cabin from the plush country club golf course. What chance did a poor Chicano with a seventh-grade education have of being welcomed in that world? Nevertheless, the boy was determined. He got a job as a gardener. Then he became a caddie. He honed his putting skills by hitting balls with a soda bottle wrapped in adhesive tape. Today, no fence keeps Lee Trevino from being welcomed into any country club in the world. Sure, Trevino had talent. But, it was not talent that kept him from quitting after he placed an embarrassing fifty-fourth in his first U.S. Open. Determination was the name of Trevino's game.

How about you? If at first you don't succeed, do you get up and try again? The difference between winners and losers is not their number of failures, but their persistence in starting again. Author Christopher Morley put it this way, "Big shots are only little shots that keep shooting."

Restore in us, O Lord, the determination
to be all we can be. Let not detours defeat us,
nor disappointments do us in.
Help us remember that we can do all things
through Christ who gives us strength. Amen.

FINISHING

It was the summer of 1968. The world had Olympic fever. The stadium in Mexico City was filled to capacity, and millions more watched by television. Trained runners from every continent crossed the finish line of the twenty-six-mile marathon. Awards were given. People's attention turned to other events. More than an hour later, a young man from Tanzania limped across the finish line. He had fallen early in the race. His knees were bleeding. His leg muscles were cramping. Dehydration was setting in. Yet he would not stop. He would not quit until he crossed the finish line. "You were injured," said the reporter in an interview, "why didn't you just quit?"

The determined runner replied, "My country did not send me five thousand miles to start the marathon. They sent me here to finish the marathon."

When it comes to the marathon of life, are you determined to finish well? Whatever the injuries, the handicaps, the setbacks, never give up, never give up, never give up.

Give us, gracious God, the courage to finish
the course, to complete the task, to accomplish
the work you have given us to do.
Let us not falter at the challenge
nor complain about the circumstances.
Rather let us run with perseverance
the race you have set before us. Amen.

PERSISTENCE

"Old man river, it just keeps rolling, it just keeps rolling along." As I floated down the river on a summer afternoon, I got to thinking about the persistence of water. It just keeps rolling along. You can't walk on water because water gives. Rather than fight back, it simply gets out of the way and down you go. Almost anything is strong enough and powerful enough to make water retreat. That's why rivers seldom run in straight lines. They are forever finding a way around their opposition. When it comes to rivers, persistence, more than power, propels them to their destination.

Could that be true of life? In our power-driven society, we assume that strength rules, the strong win, the powerful conquer. In our love of power, we are prone to disregard persistence. Perhaps it's time to take another look. "It's not by might, nor by power, but by my Spirit," says the Lord. Persistent faith, hope, and love may get us to our destination more surely than all the force in the world.

Loving God, help us find a way, everyday, help us find a way. Teach us that detours can become new directions and delays a resolve to new determination. May we reach the destination you have designed for us by whatever means available to us. Amen.

KEEP GOING

While I was enduring an extended stay in the hospital for cancer treatment, a friend sent me this quote from Winston Churchill: "If you are going through hell, keep going." The sharp statement became my motto through the long days of recovery. Life does not promise us a rose garden. Sometimes the road is hard and downright difficult. People who know pain know what I am talking about. It feels like hell!

When life dumps us in some hellish spot like that, it is important to realize that it cannot last. No problem enjoys eternal life. Every difficulty has a life span. This too shall pass. The best thing we can do for the time being is endure the present in the sure and certain hope of a better future.

So if you are going through hell, remember to keep going. Hell is no place to stop, give up, or throw in the towel. We are not meant to dwell in hell. There will be a better day. There will be a brighter tomorrow. The loving hand of the Almighty will lead you to a finer habitat. He will see you through.

Lord, when we walk through the valleys
you have promised to be with us. Help us not to
get stuck there. Take our hands, lead us on, help
us stand. Let us rise from the struggles of life
better equipped to serve you. Amen.

FRUSTRATIONS

Is something really frustrating you? Why not exploit that frustration for your future? Others have. King Gillette was tired of sharpening his straight razor, so he invented the safety razor with a disposable blade. Frederick W. Smith was fed up with slow mail, so he developed the concept of overnight delivery, which grew into Federal Express. Chester Greenwood suffered from frostbitten ears in sub-zero temperatures, so he invented earmuffs. Humphrey O'Sullivan grew tired of coming home from the print shop night after night with hurting feet from hard floors, so he affixed rubber cushions to his heels; today Humphrey O'Sullivan's rubber heels are sold all over the world.

Necessity is the mother of invention. Frustrations can lead us to new possibilities instead of high blood pressure. The next time you are faced with a problem, don't curse it, convert it. You and others will reap the benefit.

Inspire us, creative God, to transform our frustrations into something positive for ourselves and others. Place in us your creative spirit that looks so deeply into a problem, that we can discover a possibility. Let us enjoy the goodness of creation with you. Amen.

LOT IN LIFE

Somebody said the most important thing about your lot in life is whether you build on it or just use it for parking. As I observe construction around town, I'm amazed at buildings erected in unlikely places. What once seemed like wasteland can, with proper improvement, become valuable space for beautiful housing. If we can do that with land, why can't we do that with life?

"I never asked to be born!" laments Dennis the Menace in a Hank Ketchum cartoon. Technically, Dennis is right. None of us asks to be born, and few of us choose our lots in life. Life is something that happens to us. What we do with what happens to us makes all the difference.

The choice is ours. We can park on our lot in life and complain. We can ask, "Why, in the name of higher mathematics, did this lot of life fall on me?" Or we can take what is, and with grace and patience, build something beautiful for ourselves and others.

Save us, merciful God, from complaining about
our lot in life. We bring you the circumstances of
our days, asking you to transform them into acts
of praise. Give us eyes to see the possibilities
that lie at our very fingertips. Amen.

PEANUTS

Thanks to George Washington Carver, more than three hundred products are made from peanuts. Mayonnaise, cheese, chili sauce, shampoo, polish, plastics . . . the list goes on and on. Carver said it all began this way. "I was praying in the woods early one morning. I said, 'O, Mr. Creator, why did you make the universe?'"

The Creator said, "You want to know more than your mind can comprehend. Ask me something more your size." So, Carver said, "I prayed, 'Dear Mr. Creator, tell me the reason for being, the purpose of existence.'" The Creator replied, "You are still asking for more than you can handle. Cut down the extent of your request and improve the intent." So George Washington Carver said, "I asked my last question. 'Mr. Creator, why did you make this peanut?'" The Lord said, "That's better; let's get back to the laboratory and go to work!"

While we ponder the big questions of the human predicament, let us, likewise, do something positive with the possibilities at our fingertips.

Carve down the size of our requests, dear Lord,
that our small minds can comprehend the
positive things we can accomplish with the
resources you give us in life. Set us free to be all
you have made us to be,
even if it has to do with peanuts. Amen.

TAKING IT

Irving Berlin once said, "Life is 10 percent what you make it and 90 percent how you take it!" Life has its mountains; some seem too steep to climb. Life has its setbacks; some feel like fatal blows. Life has a way of asking from us more than we feel to be in us. Life can be more chance than choice, more problem than pleasure, more what happens to us than what we make happen. Of course, that's so. We did not choose to be born nor make any decision concerning the character of our families of origin. For the most part we had little input into the schools we attended, the country we inhabited, and the community in which we were raised. These are all givens.

We do, however, decide what we will do with what we have been given in the circumstances of our lives. And that, my friends, makes all the difference. Do you have what it takes to take it?

Our lives are in your hands, loving Lord.
Together we can deal with whatever comes our
way today. Give us what it takes to take it on
the roads of life, that we may live pleasing in
your sight. Amen.

ilities

VISION

A Native-American father wanted to challenge his three sons, so the legend goes. As a test, he sent them up a mountain asking each to return with a token showing how far he had climbed. The first returned with a wild flower. The father knew it flourished at the timberline. The second son returned with a red flint stone, which indicated he'd almost reached the top. After a long time, the third son returned empty-handed. "Father," said the son, "where I went there was nothing to bring back. I stood at the summit and looked out upon a valley where two rivers join an ocean."

A proud father replied, "You have nothing in your hand, but you have something even greater, you have a vision in your soul."

Are your children challenged by a vision or simply content to collect souvenirs? Are they satisfied to pick up trinkets or motivated toward a higher view? Vision is a picture of our preferred future. Without a vision, people perish. They settle for less than they really are. After all, it's the vision of the soul that makes us determined to roll toward the highest and best.

Be thou my vision, O Lord of my life.
Help me see further and reach higher
than I can imagine on my own. Give me a
picture of your preferred future and
the wisdom to pursue that possibility. Amen.

Purpose

REASON FOR LIVING

In a Tom Wilson cartoon, Ziggy is standing in front of his familiar vending machine. The sign says "Reasons for living, deposit 50 cents please."

You were created for purpose and meaning. You have a sacred design and an eternal destiny. There may be accidental conceptions, but there are no accidental births. Your siblings may wish you dead, but God has something better in mind. Even if your mother should forsake you, God will not forget you. You are always on God's mind. You are wonderfully and awesomely made.

Find your purpose for being and live into it with all your life. You can discover a life that really matters. You can make a difference in God's time. You can live, not merely survive. You can have a better life than you ever dreamed. So go for it.

You alone, loving God, can give us a life
that really matters. Let us find in you
our reason for being, our purpose for living,
and our eternal destination.
You hold our lives in your hands. Amen.

SIGNIFICANCE

Three military recruiters showed up at a high-school assembly to encourage enlistments from students. Representatives from the Army, Navy, and the Marines were each given fifteen minutes to make their presentations.

The Army and Navy recruiters got so carried away with their presentations that only two minutes remained for the Marine to make his point.

He stepped to the podium and stood absolutely silent for sixty seconds. Then he made this statement: "As I look around the room, I only see about two or three of you who could cut it in the Marines. If you think you are one of these, meet me in the cafeteria following the assembly."

Guess which recruiter's table was stormed by the students?

In an era which champions personal freedom and individual choice, have we sold commitment short? Is there a hunger in the human heart to connect with something significant, serve in a place of importance, commit to a cause that matters? I think so. And that's why God asks for all of us.

We long to be significant and accomplish
things that really matter in life, good Lord.
So guide us to make right choices,
that we can do more than simply keep busy.
Help us, instead, to make a difference
with the time we have on earth. Amen.

LEAVING A MARK

There's a law of life which says, "Everything that moves leaves its mark on the earth." Have you noticed that? Rocks tumbling down mountainsides leave scratches on other rocks. Streams leave deep scars in the soil. A tree falling in the forest breaks limbs off smaller trees as it sinks to rest. Hills and lakes are often the impressions left by moving glaciers thousands of years ago. Nothing comes or goes in the world without leaving its mark.

Criminologists tell us that no one can enter and leave a room without depositing some traces of identity—fingerprints, footprints, hairs, threads, and innumerable other clues of who we are and what we were doing. Our ability to trace a person's presence has increased greatly with improved technology.

If everything in nature—including humans—leaves a mark, what kind of mark are we leaving? Will the world be any better because we passed by?

*With your help, gracious Master, we can leave a
positive mark on the places we've inhabited.
So if there is any good we can do, any help we
can render, any difference we can make, let us
neither defer it nor neglect it, let us do it now,
for we will not pass this way again. Amen.*

WHO AM I?

Suppose a stranger walks up and asks, "Who are you?" What do you answer? You could give your name . . . but you are a lot more than a name. You could offer your occupation—doctor, lawyer, plumber, priest—but you are more than what you do for a living. You might name the school you attended, the church to which you belong, or the place you presently live—but you're a lot more than any of those.

We are complex people, and the question, "Who are you?" is not easy to answer. Most of us could use some help understanding who we really are. That's where God comes in. God knows us best and loves us most. He knitted us together in our mother's womb and even now knows the moves we make and the steps we take. The hairs on our head are numbered. The steps of our feet are directed.

You are a child of God. No less than the moon and the stars. You have a reason to be here. Remember who you are!

You knitted us together in our mother's womb,
creative God. The hairs on our head are
numbered by you. Our days are in your hands.
Make us aware of your spirit
and let us not drift away from your love.
For without you, we are nothing. Amen.

ROLLER COASTER

Richard Gregory Rodriguez rode a roller coaster for 1,013 hours over a period of forty-seven days to break his own world record. The trip left Richard with badly bruised knees, a red face that looked like a peeled tomato, and total exhaustion. Worst of all, he ended right where he started.

Many people think of life as a roller coaster ride. Life has its way of jerking us around at break-neck speeds, plunging us down hills and through tunnels until we come to a screeching halt right where we started. "Is this all there is?" we might rightfully ask as we hang on to the roller coaster rides of life.

"It need not be!" answers a voice from eternity. Life was made for investment, not entertainment. We were made for a purpose, not simply pleasure. Whether or not it is always clear to us, the winding tracks of real life lead us to an eternal destiny.

Lord, as we go round and round, up and down,
we seek for greater meaning.
You alone provide purpose in life,
you give us a reason for being.
Remind us now of that purpose and inspire us
to pursue it with all our might. Amen.

WHAT ARE WE LOOKING FOR?

A real estate agent was showing several homes to a young couple with a toddler. At each house the couple thoroughly examined each room, surveyed every closet, and opened all cabinets. The toddler followed quietly along until the couple entered the final house of the day. That's when the kid pulled the pacifier from her mouth and asked in exasperation, "What are we looking for?"

As we go from day to day, run from place to place, work from hour to hour, perhaps we need to ponder the toddler's question. What are we looking for? When we get to where we're going, where will we be? When we find what we're looking for, will we really want it?

Somebody said there are two great disappointments in life. One is not getting what you long for. The other is getting it and realizing it was not worth the effort. Do your goals have lasting values? Do your efforts make an eternal difference? Invest your life in things that never age nor lose their value.

Help us, loving God, to invest our lives in things that are everlasting. We are prone to pursue the trivial and miss the eternal, to take the cash and let the credit go. Make us wiser, blessed Lord, to the greater dimensions of life. Amen.

Relationships

AVAILABLE POWER

A little boy on a camping trip with his father was trying to move a rock to form a campfire. The kid pushed and shoved, pulled and tugged, but could not for the life of him budge the rock. The father, observing nearby, encouraged his son by saying "You can do it, you only need to use all your strength."

"I am using all my strength," the kid lamented.

"But you haven't asked me to help," replied the dad.

The lesson learned at the campfire is a lesson for us all. We struggle alone at the hard places of life oblivious to the help that is nearby. There are fathers and mothers, friends and family, and partners and professionals who are more than willing to help. They are merely waiting to be invited.

The next time you run into something you can't handle alone, don't give up. Use all your resources. With the help of people and the power of God, you can move life's most difficult mountains and find the strength to carry on.

We thank you, God, for the angels that surround us. These divine messengers are your special gifts, offering us help in time of need. Teach us to use their power to accomplish the tasks you set before us. Amen.

CONFLICTS

When it comes to conflict with people, do you tend to be a turtle, a skunk, or a real person? Turtle-like people handle conflict by staying in their shell. They hang around without sticking out their necks. They seldom make a move when anyone is around. It's hard to connect with people who relate like turtles. On the other hand, some people handle conflicts like skunks. They can't wait to spray their anger on anybody who dares to come close. The smell of their rage casts a stench on anyone around.

There are better ways to deal with our differences than becoming either skunks or turtles. Why not be real people? People do disagree. Disagreements need not be the end of the world. Through the process of assertiveness and active listening, most conflicts can be resolved to the satisfaction of all. The next time you find yourself in an argument, neither retreat to a shell nor stink up the place. Relate like a real person.

You put us in a world, dear God, with other
people. We do not always get along with one
another, so we need your intervention.
Save us from anger and retaliation
and give us the grace to forgive others
as you forgive us. Amen.

FRIENDS

After a rather unpleasant encounter with Lucy in a "Peanuts" cartoon, Charlie Brown walks away sadly muttering, "I need all the friends I can get." Me too, Charlie Brown. I need all the friends I can get.

Somebody said, "A loyal friend laughs at your jokes when they are not so good and sympathizes with your problems when they are not so bad." Friends pick us up when we are down. They hold us accountable when we run around. Friends offer help. Friends give us hope. Friends come in when the world is going out. They are the people who know us best and love us most.

Futurist John Naisbett says the more technology we introduce into society, the more people will need other people. High tech demands high touch. How are you fixed for friends? Churches provide fellowship where friendships are formed. "We share each others woes, our mutual burdens bear. And often for each other flows, the sympathizing tear."

Friend of us all, we have come to see that friends are gifts of your divine mercy. Friends double our joys and halve our sorrows. So we thank you, Divine Friend, for the gift of friendship, yours and many others. Amen.

BUMPING INTO OTHERS

Living is a contact sport. We are forever bumping into each other. Sometimes contacts make our days, like when we run into an old friend. At other times, collisions with people can hurt us, even injure us for a lifetime.

For centuries Americans avoided such collisions by creating space. Our ancestors came to America to get away from people. Our forefathers and mothers moved west to find more territory. Now, there is nowhere to run.

So the questions confront us: Can we bump into one another without a battle? Can we play on the same court without a fight?

One relational person set this for a goal, "I want to love you without clutching, appreciate you without judging, join you without invading, invite you without demanding, criticize you without blaming, and help you without insulting." Now there's the kind of person you would want to bump into.

Divine Friend, you have made us for relationships. Even when they are difficult we are better to be among others than to be left alone. We need your help when it comes to significant others. Give us the grace to bump into one another without being bruised, to come close without feeling conquered, to love without being possessed. Amen.

MORE ABOUT
FRIENDS

Somebody said friends are those rare people who ask, "How are you?" and then wait to hear the answer. How are you at forming friendships? We all need someone to lean on. Occasionally we need to lean a lot. That's not encouraging dependency; it's facing reality.

Soon after Jack Benny died, George Burns said this about him: "Jack and I were wonderful friends for fifty-five years. Jack never walked out on me when I sang a song. I never walked out on him when he played the violin. We laughed together, played together, worked and ate together. For many years we talked with each other every single day."

Friendships like that see you through. In a stepped-up, stress-filled society, it's easy to talk without listening, touch without meaning, even feel lonely in a crowded room. Friends are more than faces or even acquaintances. It takes more than a crowd to create community. It takes a friend.

What a friend we have in you, dear Jesus.
You forgive our sins, share our sorrows, and
give us grace to carry on. We have found you to
be present when others are absent.
We rejoice that nothing in all creation
can separate us from your love. Amen.

HANDS

Have you looked at your hands lately? Oh, go ahead, don't be embarrassed. Hands come in all sizes, colors, and shapes. Some are soft. Some are calloused. With a hand we can form a cup, make an arch, show a fist. Our fingers are versatile enough to lift a needle from a table or open the cap of a bottle. We are intricately and wonderfully made.

You know what I like most about hands? They touch you nicely. An extended hand of friendship on a heavy day is like water in a desert. A hand on the shoulder communicates confidence and assurance from another. The touch of a friend or lover lifts us higher than we ever thought possible.

So it comes as no surprise that we often say of life, "It's in your hands." Have you hugged your spouse today? What about your kids? In loving kindness make somebody's day with a handshake of appreciation, a backslap of encouragement, or a gentle touch of comfort.

Gentle Jesus, you used your hands
to heal the sick and comfort the lonely.
Use our hands to do your work on earth.
Let people be healed and hearts be helped
through the simple touch of kindness and the
extended hand of friendship. Amen.

TECHNOLOGY

Is modern technology helping you or hindering you? If you have a list of fifteen phone numbers to reach your family of three, your technological life may be out of control. If you have to call your son's beeper to let him know it's time to eat, and he e-mails you back from his room asking, "What's for dinner?" it may be a pretty good sign that your communication systems are out of control. If you chat several times a day with a stranger in South Africa but haven't spoken to your next door neighbor in a year, it might be time to get off the Internet.

All of us benefit from the technological advances of recent years. Most of us consider computers and cell phones essential instruments of business. But let us never forget, technology was made for humanity, not humanity for technology. There are times we need to turn off the television, shut down the computer, and get in touch with the important people of our lives.

*Teach us, Holy Spirit, the art of communication
with one another. Help us speak the truth in
love and let our yes be yes and our no be a solid
no. Make us humble in our assertions and
generous with our praise. Most of all make us
willing to listen to you. Amen.*

HUGS

A little girl insisted on hugging her dad in public. The father, a little embarrassed, said, "Stop, Beth. You're hugging me to death."

"No, Daddy," Beth explained. "I'm hugging you to life."

Studies prove Beth to be right. Menninger Foundation research reveals people need about eight hugs a day to stay emotionally comforted and secure. Hugging relieves stress, reduces pain, and helps people live longer, healthier lives. "It's a wondrous thing what a hug can do. A hug can cheer you when you're blue. A hug can say 'I love you so,' or 'Gee, I hate to see you go.' A hug can soothe a small child's pain and bring a rainbow after rain."

Have you hugged your children today? How about your husband or wife, your mother or father, your sister or brother? How about the elderly person down the street? If love is contagious, let's start an epidemic.

Dear Jesus, we have learned
to lean on your everlasting arms
and rest in the palm of your hand.
It has been sweet to walk in your caring ways
and be assured of your uninterrupted interest.
Thank you for holding us close. Amen.

MICHELANGELO

Michelangelo, so the story goes, was once seen by friends pushing a heavy rock through a village street. "Why are you laboring so over that old rock?" inquired the friends.

"Because there is an angel in there wanting to come out," Michelangelo replied.

Have you seen any angels lurking in rocks lately? There lies more beauty and strength in people around us than most of us realize. Do we have the vision and the determination to set people free? Will we help others become what they are created to be?

After all, somebody did that for you and me. A loving God created us. Determined parents raised us. All along life's way people appeared who dared to believe there was in our rocky lives something of angelic value worth setting free.

What others did for us, will we do for others? In the rocky lives of those around us, there are angels waiting to be set free.

You have made us people of great potential, cre-
ative God. Help us call forth the greatness that
lies in others hidden from normal view. Make us
instruments of your creativity,
that the necessary resources may become
available to meet the needs of the world. Amen.

MIDAS

Midas was the mythological king who had a lot of things but always wanted more. Midas asked the Greek gods to grant his greatest wish, that everything he might touch would turn to gold. The gods did. Midas touched food and it turned to gold. Midas touched furniture and it turned to gold. But when Midas touched his little daughter and she turned to gold, well, that was too much.

In our "gimme" kind of world, the legend of Midas makes a point. Do we really want God to grant all our wishes? If we do as we please, will we be pleased with what we do? Have we learned the difference between wants and needs? At what price do we work more to get more?

If we can get over the "gimmes," we might discover the joy of living and find relationships to be more precious than gold.

Save us from our addiction to things, dear Lord.
Make us mindful that people are more important
than possessions, relationships more valuable
than our reaching a goal. Help us walk gently
among all your people today and always. Amen.

RELATIONSHIPS

Two women met at a cocktail party after a separation of many years. As they exchanged greetings and caught up on old times, the first woman noticed her friend was wearing an extraordinary diamond. "That is the most beautiful and enormous diamond I have ever seen," exclaimed the woman to her friend.

"It is unusual," replied the friend. "It's the Calahan diamond. It comes complete with the Calahan curse."

"And what is the Calahan curse?" inquired the woman.

"Mr. Calahan," replied the friend.

How do you deal with the difficult people in your life? Studies show that 75 percent of us have unresolved differences with a relative or friend. In the close quarters of work and family, tempers flare, conflicts rise, and people get hurt.

What can we do? Let me mention three ideas. We can talk it out. The truth can set us free. We can love it out. Love covers a multitude of sins. We can wait it out. Walls seldom last forever.

We can love the whole world, dear Lord,
it's people who give us problems.
Since no one is perfect, teach us to deal with
everyone's imperfections—including our own.
Make us as graceful with each other's
commissions and ommissions
as you are with ours. Amen.

HOW CAN WE SAY THANKS?

How can we say thanks? Let us count some ways!

We can write a note to persons who mean the most. There are people, past and present, who have made us what we are. Family, friends, teachers, pastors, professors, and countless others. We can express our thankfulness to them.

How can we say thanks? We can express appreciation for work well done. Have you told a worker lately that you appreciate him or her? How about a waitress, a postman, a policeman, a physician, or even a public official?

How can we say thanks? We can practice random acts of kindness. We can open a door, allow a motorist to merge in traffic, smile with a child.

How can we say thanks? We can bow before our Creator and remember we are loved.

We thank you, Holy Spirit,
for your abiding presence in our lives.
You have promised never to leave us
nor forsake us, and we take comfort
in your constant care.
Wherever we wander you are there.
And that has made all the difference. Amen.

Success
& Work

ANONYMOUS

Some of life's greatest inventions and literature's finest pieces are produced by a person named Anonymous. What a debt the world owes to persons whose names have been forgotten. Who invented the wheel? Who first made use of fire? Who first pried loose a great stone lever, or dared to name the stars? Many public buildings bear important names, but others were constructed by people who remain anonymous. Many books have authors, but other names, immortal in nature, will never be placed on plaques nor found in databases. They are content to be anonymous.

Can you do good without concern for credit? Can you reach for excellence without desire for reward? Can you find a need and try to fill it without announcing that you paid for it? Anonymous. People who bear that name have more claim to fame than this world dreams of.

Is it not enough, dear Lord, that you call us by
name? We do not have to make a name for
ourselves for you have given us a name.
Help us claim our identity in you and rejoice
in your intimate knowledge of us. Amen.

127

Success

CREDIT

Did you hear about the turtle that wanted to spend the winter in Florida? Knowing he could never crawl there in time, the turtle convinced a couple of geese to help him. Each goose held the end of a rope while the turtle clinched his vise-like jaws in the center. The flight went extremely well, until someone from the ground looked up in admiration and asked, "Who thought of that?"

The turtle, unable to resist the chance to claim the credit for himself, opened his mouth and shouted, "I did."

The successful flight of many persons has resulted in a sudden fall by our similar need to claim the credit for the trip. Instead of concentrating on the destination, we become overly anxious for recognition along the road. We open our mouths too frequently and falter quite regularly. The next time you are flying high over some creative invention, just keep your mouth shut and your mind on the task. Your destination depends on it.

You give us grace, dear Lord, which is credit
where credit is not due. Fill us with your grace
that we need not be too anxious to claim the
credit even when the credit is due.
For it is enough to know you. Amen.

DASH OF LIFE

My particular profession causes me to spend a lot of time in the cemetery. I seldom visit such solemn places without reading tombstones. There are names, sometimes sayings, and usually a birth date and death date. In between those significant moments of birth and death, there lies a simple dash. One short, straight mark on the rocks of time signifying life.

None of us had much to do with our birth. It just happened to us. We may have little to do with our death. We have everything to do with that simple dash called life.

Is my life meaningful, or at least interesting and gratifying? How do I relate to significant others? Do I really live by the golden rule? What kind of reputation will I leave behind? Questions like that determine the content of life's little dash. Goodness is not a sudden blaze of glory won. It's the accumulation of days in which good deeds are done.

Day by day our lives have meaning
when we find our rest in you, loving Lord.
May we make the most of each moment
and fill each minute with purpose and meaning.
Our lives are in your hands and that
makes us feel secure. Amen.

LIMITATIONS

The legendary basketball coach John Wooden once said, "Never let what you can't do interfere with what you can do." I think that's pretty good advice, don't you?

Limitations loom before us all. There are corporate ladders that are unclimbable. There are personal dreams that remain a fantasy. There are hopes for others that will never become a reality. In spite of our best efforts, there are positions we will never fill, places we will never go, and relationships that will never materialize.

But never let what you can't do interfere with what you can do! We can do something. There are accomplishments within our reach and relationships within our grasps. There are hurts we can heal and people we can help. Some work is waiting for us to "just do it." Whatever good we can do, whatever assistance we can render, whatever difference we can make—let us neither defer it nor neglect it.

We all live handicapped lives, dear Lord.
Sometimes our limitations loom before us.
But you who created the universe out of nothing
can make something out of us.
So may we never let what we can't do
get in the way of what we can do. Amen.

MAKING A COMEBACK

Betty Hutton was a famous movie star and a huge box office attraction in the forties and fifties. But somewhere along the way, Betty Hutton got lost. Hard times came. Family problems, emotional illness, bankruptcy, depression, and alcoholism took their toll. At the end of herself, Betty Hutton found God's help and turned her life around.

She then made a comeback. She joined the cast of the Broadway musical *Annie*, playing the role of Mrs. Hennigan. At the first performance, the program notes contained extensive biographical sketches about the members of the cast, except for Betty Hutton. Under her picture there appeared only five words Betty had written. "I'm back, thanks to God."

Great comebacks create more than exciting ball games. They make great people. Is this your year for a great comeback?

Anyone in you, O Christ, is a new creation.
The old has gone the new has come.
We rejoice in your power to remake us anew.
Mold and make us after your will,
while we are waiting, yielded and still. Amen.

Work

NECESSITY

"Necessity is the mother of invention!" I've heard that all my life, haven't you? A little research proves the old saying to be absolutely true. Hanson Gregory, back in 1847, got tired of fried cakes that were soggy in the middle. So one morning Hanson removed the center before he cooked the cake, and the doughnut was created.

George Crum invented the potato chip in 1853. George was a famous chef who got angry at guests who complained about the French fries being too thick. Today, one fourth of all potatoes grown are used for potato chips.

In 1872, William Eno was attending the opera in New York City when he got stuck in one of those "after the show" traffic jams. People in horse and buggy had no traffic rules. Eno went home and designed stop signs, safety islands, and even one-way streets.

So what's bugging you? Why not put your frustration to work on some new invention? The world may be waiting for your solution.

> _Help us, redemptive Jesus, to put_
> _our frustrations into good use._
> _Never allow us to let a trouble go to waste._
> _If you could take a cross and redeem a world,_
> _surely we can take our troubles and_
> _turn them into possibilities. Amen._

SECOND CHANCE

When Thomas Edison was working on his first light bulb, he handed the finished product to a young assistant who nervously tried to carry it upstairs. And sure enough, the scared kid tripped and dropped it. The whole team had to work another twenty-four hours to make another bulb. When the historic invention was completed a second time, Edison handed the light bulb to the same young assistant who this time carried it to safety.

If at first they don't succeed, do you give people a second chance? Nobody is perfect. All of us falter and fail. Where would any of us be had not somebody believed in us enough to let us try again?

We don't need people to make excuses for us. Accountability is essential in every business, and being responsible is always the way to play the game. But as fallible human beings, we are set free to do our best, achieve our highest, and accomplish the most, when we are assured that we can keep coming back until we get it right.

You are always giving people another chance,
gracious God. Teach us to be like you.
May we not only receive mercy
but extend mercy wherever mercy is needed.
Freely we have received.
Let us freely give. Amen.

SOMETHING FOR NOTHING

Once upon a time there was man who found a five dollar bill on the ground. He felt so lucky that he spent the rest of his life looking down. Over the years, he collected 29,516 buttons, 54,172 pins, pennies, and pieces of string. He also gained a bent back and a miserable attitude, all because he spent his life trying to get something for nothing.

There is a growing mentality in our day that seems to say, "It's better to be lucky than productive." The big break, the lucky win, and the crucial play have replaced our commitment toward an honest day's work for an honest day's pay. Maybe luck has even overtaken faith as a modern-day religion.

Life has its free gifts. There's the glory of a sunrise, the shimmer of an evening star, the beauty of a snowfall, and the wonder of blue skies. These are not reserved for the lucky. They are God's free gifts to all. For the rest of our desires, why not take what we need and learn to pay for it?

*Lord, you have promised to supply all our needs
according to your riches in glory.
Help us to enjoy the gifts of sunrises and
snowflakes, life for today and hope for
tomorrow. As for the rest, let us travel lightly
so we may live joyfully. Amen.*

A STEADY HAND

There's an old saying which goes, "A brimming cup requires a steady hand." While it takes a lot of skill to "make it," it takes a lot of steadiness to handle "having it made."

How many people do you know who've self-destructed at the best moments of their lives? Couples stick together during the long haul of education on limited resources, but fall apart at the very moment they earn their degrees. People persevere on the long climb of the corporate ladder, then trip and fall near the top. Behind closed doors, executives sit lonely wondering if this is really all there is. Success can be harder to handle than failure.

If getting all you've ever wanted has left you feeling shaky, let the Lord of the universe steady your hand. The peace he provides passes all understanding.

Steady us, O Lord, on the journey of life,
that we may rest in your peace and enjoy
your consolations. Let us not grow weary
in well doing but confidently acknowledge you
through all our days and in all our ways. Amen.

STUCK

A tractor trailer rig got stuck under an overpass. A large crowd gathered to watch as the driver struggled to pull it free. He put the rig in low, but the trailer wouldn't budge. He put the truck in reverse, shoved the pedal to the metal, but the trailer never moved. When the frustrated trucker rolled out of the cab, a small boy stepped out of the crowd.

"I think I can help," said the kid to the trucker.

"Just what could you do about it?" snapped the driver.

"I'd let the air out of the tires," said the boy. "That would free the trailer; you could drive out and refill the tires."

Maybe that kid's advice is good for life. When we get stuck in some overpass of our own making, we will do well to stop, let the air out of our inflated egos, back up a step or two, and refill the space of our lives with wisdom and devotion. We can begin again. Success does not belong to those who never fail. Success belongs to those who, having failed, find the courage to learn from their mistakes, and try again.

Humble us, Lord, by your mercy, that we
may travel through life freely,
avoiding the pitfalls caused by an inflated ego.
Help us trust in you instead of
leaning on our own understanding.
Grant us mercy when we miss the mark of your
high calling and forgive us, we pray. Amen.

WORK

C. S. Lewis once described hell as a place where everyone is perpetually concerned about their own advancement and self-importance. It's a place where everyone wishes everyone else's demotion and ruin, where "dog eat dog" and "stab in the back" are the agendas of the day. Have I just described your work environment?

Work consumes a major portion of our lives. It takes our time and finest devotion. But it does not have to be hell on earth. If we want people to do their best and accomplish their finest, we will each do our part to make work a place of hospitality and congeniality. Work is no place to choose sides and create losers. Work is a place for joint victories and shared defeats. Work is a place where people are respected and the golden rule is practiced. Are you treating people at work the way you would like to be treated?

Teach us, gracious God, to practice our faith
in the workplaces of our lives.
In the routines of the day,
let grace abound and love be found.
May we do unto others today, what we
would have them do unto us. Amen.

Values
& Truths

RELIGION IN AMERICA

According to a survey of religion in America, the numbers of people who trust in God, believe in miracles, and pray daily have grown by double digits in the last ten years. Americans worship twice as often as the French or British. We continue to be a nation in touch with its soul.

Rightly so. With statements of faith carved in our public buildings and inscribed on our coins, can we ever doubt the dimensions of belief that guided our forefathers and mothers? Faith can form a solid foundation for us, too. There are guiding principles to evaluate our technological advancements. There are sacred vows which form our family covenants. There are basic values which empower human relationships. The abiding light of such principles, covenants, and values will guide us rightly, too.

Good Lord, you have given us principles
by which your world will work.
It is not lack of knowledge but feebleness of will
that confuses us. Rebuild the foundations of
faith among us, that we will not falter
along the road of life. Amen.

THE BEST OF LIFE

I buried a friend of mine one day. He died of cancer. He was fifty-eight. During the dark nights of a deadly disease, my friend made this discovery: The end of life is the best of life.

Priorities and purpose, and relationships and religion find their focus when life is threatened. For years and years we go our merry ways and live our hectic lives. There are places to go, things to do, appointments to keep, ambitions to fulfill. Then, sudden as a shell screaming out of the night, we discover our days are numbered. The heart fails. The cancer grows. The accident happens. There, in despair, comes a great revelation . . . keeping busy can be replaced with really living.

That's what my friend discovered. His family grew closer. His faith grew deeper. His life reached out to touch a wide circle of people suffering with similar disease. Instead of cursing God and dying, he praised God and started living.

Day by day, dear Lord, you give us
the gift of life. Not even death
can separate us from your love.
So help us live each moment and
love each moment as if it were our
last day on earth. And when our work here
is done, lead us gently home. Amen.

PRIORITIES

U.S. Air Force Captain Scott O'Grady was shot down over Bosnia back in the summer of 1995. For six days O'Grady managed to evade capture, subsisting on a diet of leaves and insects. Then, in a daring rescue operation, marine helicopters returned him to safety.

Captain O'Grady, reflecting on that experience, says, "My life priorities were slapped into line during those six days. I came to realize that only three things were important in this world. Number one was faith in God, the source of all goodness. Number two was the love of family and friends. And number three was good health. Beyond that everything was negotiable."

Sooner or later all of us decide what really matters in this life. Intentionally or haphazardly, our lives reflect the decisions we make. Have you learned to sort the urgent from the important in your life?

Creator God, you created us with
the ability to choose. We claim that gift
as a part of our humanity. Since there is more to
do today than we can accomplish,
make us wise in the choices we make.
Teach us to set priorities according to
your plan for our lives. Amen.

ABSOLUTES

A troubled music major sat in her professor's office lamenting life's lack of certainty. Her childhood faith was being challenged by higher education and, worst of all, her boyfriend had just dropped her. Life was leaving her shaky to say the least. The two of them talked for a while, then the wise professor walked over to the tuning fork suspended by a cord and struck it with a mallet. "That, my friend, is an A," said the professor. "It was an A all day yesterday and it will be an A all day tomorrow. In fact, it will still be an A next week and whoever strikes it a thousand years from now will still hear the sound of an A."

In the shifting sands of time, perhaps we would be wise to sound the sure and certain truths that are the same yesterday, today, and forever. God is good. Life is precious. People are important. Morals do matter. Truth is triumphant.

Jesus, you are the same, yesterday, today,
and forever. In the changing scenes of time
you remain constant. Teach us to take our
direction from you. Let us not waver with the
courses of history. Let us find
our true direction in you. Amen.

Wisdom & Prudence

FOG

Cruising down the highway recently I ran into a patch of fog. It was thick and dense. I couldn't see five feet in front of me. Motorists braked quickly, creating a hazard of their own. Lights came on. Time ticked by. The only way to get through the fog was to slow down, be careful, and take it easy.

I find life to be foggy at times, too. How about you? For a while we sail along sunshiny days. But not always. Clouds gather. Fog settles. The road becomes dark. It's hard to find the way.

Such times demand we slow down, turn on our lights, watch carefully, and proceed patiently. Fog does not last forever. Fog is something you go through. It lifts. The sun shines. Life returns to normal. We see clearly enough to resume our regular speed. On the road of life, as surely as interstates, drive carefully through the fog.

Lord, we do not always know where we are
going. It is hard to find our way through the fog.
So let us walk by faith when we cannot walk by
sight, in the sure and certain hope that
you will lead us to the light. Amen.

EDISON

As a child, Thomas Edison was anything but brilliant. One teacher described him as addled. In reality, he was a slow, systematic thinker who never relied on luck. He had a thousand experiments that failed before he succeeded in inventing the light bulb. Success, according to Thomas Edison, was 1 percent inspiration and 99 percent perspiration.

The story of Edison is repeated often. The best students in college are not always the most brilliant. They are focused persons who are determined to get an education. The most successful employees are not always the brightest minds on the block. They are committed persons who are willing to concentrate on the task until it is completed.

Intelligence is a gift distributed in varied proportions to human beings. Wisdom is the creative use of that gift. Wise people are able to focus their energies on a specific goal until the task is accomplished—even if it takes a thousand attempts.

Fill us with determination, loving God, that we may accomplish the work you have given us to do. May we not falter before the task is finished nor despair in the duties of the day. Keep us working in your will and in your way. Amen.

IF IT FEELS GOOD

Do you remember learning to ride a bicycle? One person described it this way: "About a mile from our house the road went down a steep hill and turned sharply at the bottom. The first time I road a bicycle over that hill, the gathering speed left me ecstatic. To give up this ecstasy by the application of brakes seemed absurd. So I let it go. My ecstasy ended seconds later when I was propelled a dozen feet off the road into the woods. I was badly scratched and bleeding. The front wheel of my bike was twisted beyond use. By refusing to limit my ecstasy, I had lost my balance and wrecked my bike."

If it feels good, do it! Is that your motto for life? Who needs a brake when the ride seems so thrilling? Who wants to limit the ecstasy of the experience? Why slow down, back off, think it over, or proceed with caution when the ride itself is a high? Why? Because life, like roads, has curves. Those who lose their balance are bound to crash.

Lord, you have set us free not to do as we please
but to do as you will. Place in us the checks and
balances that will protect us on the roads of life.
Help us know when to let go and
when to slow down. Amen.

JUMPING TO
CONCLUSIONS

A middle-aged man entered a cocktail lounge and walked directly to the bar. "Do you have anything that will cure hiccups?" he asked the bartender. Without saying a word, the bartender reached under the bar, picked up a wet rag, and slapped the man across the face with it. The stunned man exclaimed, "Hey, what's the big idea?"

The bartender smiled, "Well, you don't have the hiccups anymore, do you?"

Wiping his face the man replied, "I never did have the hiccups. My wife has the hiccups. She's waiting outside in the car."

Jumping to conclusions is the most exercise a lot of people get. Conclusions stem from facts, reason, evaluation, decision. When we fail to follow that process, we are likely to offer the right remedy to the wrong person. The next time you are tempted to offer solutions without considering the situation, stop, look, and most of all, listen.

Loving Savior, we not only make mistakes we are often downright wrong. We have jumped to conclusions that will not stand the test of time. Forgive us, we pray. Open our minds to new possibilities, that we may grow in the art of wisdom. Amen.

Prudence

SMART

A recent graduate facing the real world for the first time lamented to a friend, "I'm not as smart as I thought I'd be." Maybe that young adult had gained a heart of wisdom as well as a head full of information.

It is a great moment in our lives when we discover we are not as smart as we once thought ourselves to be. The salesperson who makes manager, the accountant who is now the controller, the vice president who is approached for the presidency—all who have won their status by honest commitment and tireless dedication know in their hearts they are not as smart as they thought they would be.

Such recognition of reality is a worthy development of wisdom. They are people willing to learn, seek advice, and improve with time.

So, if you are not as smart as you thought you would be, you are probably wiser than you realize.

We confess to you, O God, that we
are not as smart as we would like to be.
We would like to understand
the mysteries of the universe.
Instead we search for enough wisdom
to get us through the day.
In your mercy, may that be enough. Amen.

STRESS

A national magazine sent a photographer to take pictures of a forest fire. The photographer was to meet a small plane at a private airport, which would fly him to the site. The photographer arrived at the airport late, and seeing a small Cessna airplane, jumped in and said, "Let's go." A tense pilot turned the plane into the wind and they were off. "Fly over the north side and make a low pass over the fire," instructed the photographer.

"Why do that?" inquired an even more nervous pilot.

"Because I'm a photographer," said the passenger. "I need to get low to take good pictures."

A now extremely frightened pilot replied, "You mean you're not the flight instructor?"

Actions taken under stress can leave any of us in a heap of trouble. Taking time to ask the right questions in order to make the right decisions is essential in human survival.

Save us, gracious Lord, from running
past more than we catch up with.
In the rush of life, slow us down so we may gain
eternal perspective on temporal things.
Grant us the marvelous gift of wisdom. Amen.

Prudence

TRY SMARTER

Try smarter, not harder—have you considered that solution to your latest pressure? There is a myth in American society that any task can be accomplished if enough effort is applied. Believers in this myth move mountains by shoveling harder. They are usually lonely people who feel the responsibility of making things happen. They are people who used to take a day off, have time for family, attend worship, or talk with their neighbors. Now they just stay busy shoveling harder. Society even encourages them with a few bronzed souvenir shovels to hang on their office walls.

One such shoveler, however, made this discovery. "He who is already in a hole should stop digging." That's another way of saying that things do not always get better by trying harder. They could even get worse. So, the next time you dig your way into a hole too deep to handle, stop, step back, and assess the situation. Try smarter instead of harder. It could make all the difference.

Dear Lord, we remember that it is not by might,
nor by power, but by your Spirit
that your kingdom comes on earth.
Remind us that we cannot do it all ourselves,
nor need we try. So help us to be as graceful
with ourselves as you are with us. Amen.

WISDOM

Dennis the Menace, in a Hank Ketchum cartoon, explains wisdom this way: "My Grandpa says you learn most everything after you think you know it all." After you think you know it all, you discover drinking and driving don't mix. After you think you know it all, you discover life is fragile. After you think you know it all, you find relationships are more important than accomplishments. Ah, the lessons to be learned after we think we know it all.

Wisdom is not a matter of earning degrees nor does it automatically come with age. Wisdom is internalizing the great truths of life. Wise people consider the consequences of certain actions. Wise people consider the eternal dimensions of temporal decisions. Wise people know they are not the only persons on this planet nor do they have the final word on any subject under the sun. It takes humility and determination to become wise.

So, how about it? How much have you learned since you knew it all?

Wise and wonderful God, you hold the universe
together and direct the paths of your people.
We would like to know more than we do.
Perhaps it is enough to put our trust in you.
So guide us, great Jehovah. Amen.

Prudence

MOUNTAINS AND
MOLEHILLS

Somebody said the greatest cause of ulcers is mountain climbing over molehills.

Every problem that arises does not qualify as a crisis. Most situations are not life and death matters. For many years I served as a volunteer on a county rescue squad. We were responsible for the ambulance service to the area. My Emergency Medical Training had me believing all calls were critical. Experience exposed a different story. There were occasional cardiac arrests, but most runs called for Band-Aids™, not brain surgery.

All life situations call for evaluation before excitement. A misunderstanding between friends need not be the end of a relationship. A child's bad grade in school does not make the child a bad person. A dip in the stock market does not mean financial disaster. A conflict in marriage need not mean a collapse of the covenant. We are better equipped to handle real emergencies when we know the difference between mountains and molehills.

Lord, things are not always what they
sometimes seem to be. So make us wise in
assessing situations, that we may be successful
in solving the problems of life.
Remind us that no problem is facing us today
that we cannot handle by your grace. Amen.